POLITICAL ECONOMY OF UNDERDEVELOPMENT OF NORTH–EAST INDIA

POLITICAL ECONOMY
OF
UNDERDEVELOPMENT
OF
NORTH–EAST INDIA

Rafiul Ahmed
Prasenjit Biswas

AKANSHA PUBLISHING HOUSE
NEW DELHI-110 059 (INDIA)

AKANSHA PUBLISHING HOUSE
R 37-B, Vani Vihar, Uttam Nagar
New Delhi-110059
Email: ektabooks@yahoo.com
Ph. : 56065579 / 9811582579

Political Economy of Underdevelopment of North-east India

First Edition 2004
ISBN 81–87606–39–8

PRINTED IN INDIA

Published by M.P. Misra for Akansha Publishing House, New Delhi and Printed at Tarun Offset Press, Delhi.

For My Friend
and
Philosopher
TAUHID

There Was Life There One, and Joy in Recreation,
Dancing and Laughter, Love Among The Trees,
But Little Now Save Sullen Speculation
Of What the Future Has and Where it Leads

—Verrier Elwin (1902-64)

Preface

The problem of Underdevelopment in North-East India (NEI) assumes a complex political and cultural form. In concrete Political Economy terms development is both related to a prevalent mode of production as well as reproduction of social relations of production. Therefore, the political economy of underdevelopment takes into account the social relations of production and its genesis in a given system of production. NEI being the cultural and economic periphery of India's mainland exhibit relationship of dependency between the modes of production prevalent in NEI and the modes of production prevalent in the larger domain of India's economy. The clinching evidence for this dependency relation lies in the fact that NEI acts as a supplier of raw material for the mainland and in turn receives investment in finished goods from the mainland. This process of resource use and expansion of market to NEI results into a grand process of social and political homogenization. But economic processes cannot fully appropriate NEI into the fold of Indian market rather it increases the already existing social and cultural differentiation by way of developing neo-elites as the allies of Indian Capital. This relationship with the Indian Capital does not ensure the self-determination of NEI. Rather it provides the space for operation of the Indian Capital.

This instrumental rendering of NEI into an ally and a supportive market of Indian Capital gives rise to dominant ideology of subsumption of regional identities within the fold of the national pan-Indian identity. But such subsumption produces its own antithesis in the form of assertion of multiple smaller ethnic and linguistic identities that clamor for their distinct self-definition and politico-territorial self-determination. This shows that politically constructed identities resist the processes of dominance and homogenization. Such resistance is articulated in praxis and in actual struggle for survival and sustenance. In terms of 'Political Economy', with the rise of dependency between NEI and the mainland India, there has been a corresponding rise of resistance as its dialectical counterpart.

In the case of NEI the most important and major linguistic identity is the *Assamese* identity but in a narrow sense such identities are resistant as well as yielding. The construction of *Bodo* identity for e.g. would mobilize the support of *Bodo* ethnic elites while it could not master support from civil society in Assam in general. This work takes into account how such identities represent live the conflicts endemic in the structure and how the structure of reproduction shape identities that are in a state of conflict and contest.

Further it is argued that what follows from dependency relationship is a subperpherialization i.e., creation of peripheries within peripheries. As these periperipheries within peripheries stand in a dialectical relationship with peripheries that play the role of local centers, there is a privileged positioning of social identities in those centers, from where they extend their influence on subperipheries. On the one hand such identities draw their Counterhegemonic strength by moving against the metropolitan centers while they would extend their hold on their immediate neighbourhood. As resources would move from subperipheries to local centers and from local centers to metropolitan centers, formation of identities act as a linkage as well as sever the linkage between subperiphery and metropolitan centers of India. This simultaneous linkage and delinking between subperipheries and metropolis could be conceived as a form of *neo-dependency* that allows subperipheries a relative autonomy and draw from them and yet extend its influence on subperipheries to maintain a permanence of the process of surplus extraction.

Rafiul Ahmed
Prasenjit Biswas

Acknowledgements

The pursuit of the ideas in this work owes a great deal to our teachers, friends and well-wishers. The Department of Humanities and Social Sciences, I.I.T., Mumbai, proved to be a congenial and tolerant home for us to carry out research in a multidisciplinary field. Travelling requires that the pilgrim be well prepared for the arduous and unknown nature of the journey. In this task we owe sincere gratitude and respect to our teachers. Prof. Biswas taught me philosophy and a great deal more. Prof. Ramanathan has influenced us substantially to arrive at quite a few insights in relation to practical aspects of development. Especially in matters of pursuing and choosing ideas the experience of learning from Prof. Ramanathan, I believe, has not only helped us for the book but also gave us a long way to go. Prof. Malshe and Prof. Subudhi have been a constant encouragement, gave us good advice and took critical interest throughout the study. They have spared no effort in the careful questioning and articulation of idea in this work. Our friends Subash and Sheshagiri have been a perfect agent provocateur, and helped enormously through their interest in our study. Upendra, Abhilash and Omkumar have the most kind and helpful in reviewing the manuscript. Of course, while I owe much, all errors and misinterpretations are our own responsibility.

Finally, we all hear about the magic moments of MPhil. (Planning and Development) when for a time economists, geographers, sociologists and people from other background come together around central issues and common questions. At those times, the spirit of inquiry kindles the spirit of discovery. In this process many are involved, only few can be explicitly acknowledged, but all can be thanked.

Rafiul Ahmed

Prasenjit Biswas

Contents

1

Introduction, the Problem and Approach

Introduction

The North-East India (NEI) lies in the cultural periphery of India and it is a distinctive region in terms of its physiography, climate, topography, vegetation and social and cultural formations. The whole region is situated between the 69 degree 40 E and 97 degree 37 E and is connected with rest of India by a narrow strip of land through northern part of Bengal. Based on the physical features the regions embody mountains, hills and plateaus. The sub-tropical location of the region gives rise to different kinds of flora and fauna. The Monsoon showers almost all parts of the region. As the subsistence agriculture depends heavily on the Monsoon it can be called as the backbone of the economy. Agriculture is the prime activity and major contributor to the economy of North- East states but it is not highly mechanized. The region is one of the most industrially backward regions. In the presence of several constraints it has not been able to contribute significantly to the domestic production. Although the region shows tremendous multiplicity in terms of language, caste, race, religion, ethnic groups there are common features, which is distinctive from the rest of the country. The tribal people dominate the hilly area while the non-tribal people dominate the valleys. Most of the states of the NEI have high percentage of tribal population. However one cannot compare them with the traditional stereotype found in the mainland. For example Mizos have achieved high literacy rate of (90%). The centripetal and the centrifugal forces have shaped the Polity of the region historically. However, in the case of NEI there has been a predominance of the former on the later. In this beautiful corridor between two great civilizations of the Chinese and the Indian, the creative endeavors of generations of people of this enchanted land have strengthened the forces of pluralism and fusion of harmony among the forces of different faiths. The diverse ethnic origins of the people inhabiting this difficult and tortuous terrain naturally led to the growth of centrifugal forces, directly stemming from various ways of living, different forms of worship and separate dialects. Over the years, there emerged a cultural commonality, which greatly contributed to the social cohesion. The Eastern Himalayas and the river Brahmaputra has greater influence on the life of the people of the region. The legends, myths, folklores and the customs of the area are woven with those of the rest of India as they developed cross-cultural communication.

What is culturally important about the region is a tremendous diversity of languages and dialects estimated at some 400 odd numbers. The linguistic origins could be traced back to the Indo-Austric, Mon Khmer, Indo-Tibetan, Tibeto Burman and of course Indo-Aryan group of languages. The linguistic diversity of the region is the root of the ethnic diversity. The ethnic diversity could be charted out in roughly 120 scheduled tribes in the region, while the each of these tribes have several sub-tribes, clans and kinship ties. The linguistic and ethnic diversity assumes an architectonic form, as one can trace a continuum from clan to tribe to ethnicity to nationality. For example major tribes of the region bear a generic name such as *Naga*, *Mizo* etc. *Naga* in particular comprises of some 22 sub-tribes, each of which could again be divided into clans and kinship markers. *Mizos* too consider themselves as a part of larger generic identity called 'Zo' which is constituted by tribes who trace their origin to *Sinlung,* a place somewhere in south-west China. Apart from such ethnic configurations by the tribes, ethnicity also comprise of generic linguistic and religious identity. The generic linguistic identity called Assamese connotes sharing of Assamese language by *Vaishnavaites*, *Sankardevaites*, *Muslims*, *Ahoms*, and migrants, hill and plain tribes of Assam all coalesced into the name Assamese. Each such generic members, therefore, has a substratum of plurality and diversity that cohere but do not collapse the specific terms of reference.

Such a diversity has given rise to historical and political forces that mutually collaborate and contradict yet preserve the substratum of diversity in a holistic presence of region. During the pre-colonial, colonial and the post-colonial period there have been state formations of distinct kinds. Three dominant models during pre-British were 1) politics that followed Hinduism as the religion of 'royal legitimation' e.g. *Meitees*, *Jaintias*, *Dimasas* and *Tripures*, *Chakmas*, etc. 2) The Buddhist polities such as *Chakmas*, *Khamtis*, *Nokte*, *Dukpa* etc. 3) The tribals and animist polities such as Ahoms and Khasis. The institutions of chieftainship also prevailed among a number of incipient state formations such as *Lushai, Angami*, *Konyak*, *Aos* and others. Such diverse political formations of the pre-colonial era presented a difficult situation. When the Britishers intended to establish their governance in NEI what they did was to establish an umbrella authority over the local institutions of rule throughout the first and second half the nineteenth century. The British state followed a pattern of punitive expedition in the case of tribes of Naga and Mizo Hills. In the case of plains of Assam it established the headquarters of the government around 1826 from where it extended its areas of influence. But the bottom line of British administration was non-interference in the social modes of tribal life. This British policy amounted to an indirect rule whereby the British authorities acted as a mediating agency and established a kind of regulative authority over the hill tribes of North-East India.

This policy of non-interference resulted into a two-fold political process. On one the hand it allowed the freedom of conducting the affairs of tribal life to the tribes themselves. On the other hand it imposed a kind of strict neutrality on the British state. Such a mix between autonomy to the tribals and neutrality of the British state avoided the path of confrontation and it prevented the influence of mainstream political movement on the hill tribes.

The British regime established Inner Line Regulation over Mizoram, Meghalaya, Nagaland and Arunachal Pradesh in 1872-73. This Inner Line Regulation got further legitimized in government of India Act of 1935 which divided the whole hill areas of NEI into 'excluded' and 'partially excluded' categories. The purpose of such restrictive regulation was to ensure non-interference from people of the plains as well as carve out an area of unimpeded self-development for the tribes of the regions. The post-colonial Indian state continued with the Inner Line Regulation within the Nehruvian policy framework, which also has a component of leaving the tribes themselves. What is to be noted here is that starting from pre-colonial era to colonial and post-colonial era there has been recognition of specific tribal and ethnic identities through the policies of the state. But such a policy was not complemented with adequate support of capability building in the region. Rather the policy of pursuing development through political concessions and funding from the Centre have drawn the region into the fold of nation-building process that sharpened the difference and unevenness between levels of progress as obtained at the national and the regional plane.

Looking into the contemporary forms of social and political struggle emerging from NEI one would surmise about some of the major problems that inflict the region. Located in a complex geo-political interface the region has been affected by the demographic consequences of partition. The steady flow of immigrants and refuges across the border resulted into a kind of ethnic outburst throughout 60s and 70s. One of the running themes of ethnic struggle of the region is devoted to the influx of foreigners, which has been made into the cause for development at lacks. Further, the issue of influx has been pitted against the problem of inequitable distribution and thereby such an issue thwarted more urgent issues of economic struggle. The ever-widening class difference and dis-empowerment of rural and tribal masses and the backwash effects of development in the metropolis were stumped under the bogie of influx and thereby hampering the processes of cultural integration. One would further say that lack of development compounded with ethnic difference posed severe constraint on the possibilities of attaining legitimate political and economic aspirations towards which ethnic mobilization were directed to. Such non-fulfillment of various legitimate concerns alienated large sections of ethnic communities of NEI. It clearly demonstrate the fact that the Nehruvian policy leaving them alone did not ensure appropriate self-development. So also the role of the Indian State was far less than satisfactory.

The administration of welfare throughout the functioning of various state and local level institutions assumed an elitist and bureaucratic form. Assam, the largest conglomeration of hill and plane areas were had to be divided into other smaller states as it was not possible to fulfill the minimal aspirations of various ethnic communities. Mizo Hill District experienced terrible famine between 1952-56 giving rise to three decade long insurgency. Such insurgencies have forced the Indian State to carve out areas of Assam and states like Nagaland (1963), Mizoram and Meghalaya (1972) were created. Such carving out of the states was a restatement of self-development for the tribes, but the machinery and the state governance could not fully attain such a goal. Especially the goal of welfare could not have been achieved with underutilization of funds and resources leading to a kind of underdevelopment of such newly formed states. The governmental machinery created only a top-down administration within which the local self-governance and traditional institutions of various tribes could retain a nominal presence. Rather it gave rise to an intense conflict between traditional institutions and state government leading to an unaccountable condition of development.

If one looks into the environmental niches that traditionally sustained the livelihood practices of the various tribes of the region one would encounter a conflict between nature and culture. While ethnographers and anthropologist have emphasized on preservation of ethnic and natural styles of living, the politicians and planners have asked for larger public investments. There were clear divergences of goals, whether to pursue the path of model institutional development or strengthen the resource bases of the communities became an either-or question. As the choice of development was not left to the people themselves but was delivered by the statist agencies it has led to an absence of well-defined goals of development. The whole of the region promises to hold indigenous ways of development that are somehow scuttled and continued by various exogenous forces. As the resource base of the region is gradually weaned away it had produced a displacement of communities from their life world while introduction of various other ways of life could not involve a sustainable process of balanced growth.

Political Economy of Underdevelopment

Modes of Production and Development

Patnaik (1973) in his article "On the Political Economy of Underdevelopment" sheds light on the development of capitalistic economy in the Indian subcontinent and the concomitant process of accumulation thus creating development in the metropolis and underdevelopment in the periphery. In this exclusive paper Patnaik not only traces the historical genesis of underdevelopment and the process of capitalistic development but also the contradictions generated as a result of the dissolution of the old mode of production.

He argues in the essay that capitalistic development took place in India essentially through the process of primary accumulation. It was mainly by appropriating petty producers of a particular group in whose hands the means of production and subsistence were accumulated and the large masses were left to sell their labour power. A market was provided for the products of the new mode within which "these two groups came face to face." Historically, this happened through a process in which the pre-capitalistic producers were separated from the means of production and a process of appropriation or possession by a few the things so appropriated.

This process of "primary accumulation" involved the state apparatus and the use of force to set the mode of production on its feet and simultaneously to provide it with a market. Once on its feet, the capitalistic production relied to greater extent on internal appropriation of surplus value. Primary accumulation in one sense continued side-by-side with accumulation and production for internal market, which petty producers have expropriated continuously. The chief motive force behind the capitalistic production relied on three elements i.e. accumulation, concentration and centralization.

The offshoot of the above process gave rise to two separate tendencies; firstly, the constant expropriation of the many by few created a "surplus population", a mass of unemployed and underemployed pauperized producers, secondly, the capital developed by this process tended to be geographically unevenly distributed owing to the existence of "external economies". Thus the overall impact of the process was underdevelopment in the periphery and development in the metropolis; the later characterized by integration into world trade as primary producers and the existence of a "surplus population" which had to survive at its best it could. This entire process of development and underdevelopment took place at an international level through the medium of a colonial state or "comprador state".

However, liberation movement challenged this pattern of change in the "peripheral" countries, in many of which the national bourgeoisie emerged as the dominant force. In its effort to start an indigenous capitalistic development the "national bourgeoisie" faced certain unique problems –i) it had no colonies left to acquire ii) simultaneously having been colonized it inherited a far poorer country. The population growth was constantly making matters worse iii) it also arrived at a time when the world capitalistic system was politically challenged iv) finally with all this failings, the liberation movement could not make it capable of the task.

At this juncture, Patnaik argues that the "national bourgeoisie" because of these drawbacks allied itself with the landlords and after some patchy land reforms settled down to the business of providing a sort of "rural capitalism" from above. However, the typical political instinct of "national bourgeoisie" precluded it to take bold measure like using vast mass of unutilized labour for capital formation. As the surplus value generated within the tiny capitalistic sector was inadequate, primary accumulation had to supplement it and took the form of drastic squeeze on the consumption of the masses i.e. the labourers. Moreover, where the resulting development was concentrated in a certain region, the old metropolis-periphery relationship was reproduced within the country.

What stands out is that with the rising consumption of the bourgeoisie and the landlords the primary accumulation became inadequate and capital had to be borrowed from metropolitan centres. As a result, the national bourgeoisie had to realign itself with the metropolitan bourgeoisie soon after the independence on different terms and different levels. The continued borrowing sapped the foundation of the bourgeoisie programme of independent national development. It was under pressure to dismantle the system of trade and foreign capital, which had developed since independence and in several cases, succumbed to the pressure at least partially. The same contradictions can also be drawn from the political developments wherein on one hand the government talks about the opening up of the economy to the market forces and in another hand it makes legislation for the decentralization of the planning process.

What emerges from this global political economy of Underdevelopment is the systemic growth of peripheries and a steady process of accumulation at the cost of peripheries that not only happened internationally, but also was supplemented within a geopolitical region, reproducing and mimicking what happened at the global scale. But one has to understand the specifics of Capital formation and especially how formation of capital brought in a regimen of control over factors of production.

Bagchi (1998) makes an attempt to analyses the nature of colonial enterprises in India in order to trace the processes of primary accumulation and its impact on labourers who constitute the "subjects" of development. Bagchi presents the cases of indigo cultivation, sugar industry and the textile industry during the colonial period in India, where he witnessed retardation of productive forces and relative emboldening of the regressive labor process. He identifies coercive labour employment as the prominent feature of capitalistic enterprise in

India. In this process all the players such as the British govt., the Zamindars and the moneylenders acted harmoniously. Not only this, other factors like relative roles of ideology, clan systems and the market system played important role in maintaining the super ordinate force of sahibs on sustaining the coercion of the laborers. This very system of joint coercion and subsequent destruction of alternative employment opportunities had a depressive effect on the forces of production. The whole mechanism reduced the nominally free peasants to a condition of abject dependence on the *Zamindars* and the European planters.

The influence of colonialism went beyond the coercive method of labour control. In case of manufacture of textiles influence of colonialism and land-lordism was felt in the behavior of labour, choice of technique and the spread of adoption and diffusion of technical change. The very methods of labour control –physical coercion, intimidation by jobbers and the absorption of the superior powers in every way to the colour of the skin militated against many needed changes, such as the induction of the technically qualified Indians in supervisory positions.

The nature of capitalistic enterprise is not just bound by coercion, but also is based on the ideological underpinnings involved in strengthening or undermining the existing power relations of the producers in general in the countryside in different regions of India. With reference to this particular point he feels that to answer this ideological and institutional aspects of the working of colonialism in tandem with the residues, transformers or surrogates of the pre-colonial heritage in all relevant areas to be studied together with the single fact of colonialism in India as a system of exploitation of people of a geographically defined area with definite ethnic and cultural characteristics.

Both Bagchi's and Patanaik's works find their reverberations in Amaledu Guha's *Planter's Raj to Swaraj*(1977) that deals with the dominant labour processes of migratory labour forces, who are put to the task of running Capitalist tea enterprises in large areas of North East India. The work clearly shows that how the tea industry drew upon the labour force from the regions of the country which are impoverished due to surplus extraction and primary accumulation. Further Guha showed how extraction of surplus from tea industry resulted into a kind of pre-capitalist production relation between planters and labourers extended to other sectors of the economy by the British State. So tea industries as colonial capitalist enterprises established a pre-capitalist mode of exploitation of labour, while it produced surplus for the whole of colonial state. One can add to the study made by Sanjib Baruah in his piece entitled, "Clash of Resource Use Regimes in Colonial Assam: A Nineteenth Century Puzzle Revisited" shows how transfer of surplus of the tea industry to the mainland and further to England resulted into a severe contradiction between *two* types of resource use: *gathering of natural resources* by the indigenous people of the region versus *settled cultivation used for transfer of resources for economic purposes* giving benefits to settlers. Such settled cultivation that had existed in tea cultivation subsequently got extended to all areas of cultivation. As a result the concept of a settled workforce and the rationale of making profits through commercial transfer of resources caused a premature annihilation of shifting cultivation of the pre-colonial days and introduced new relations of production between settlers and settled cultivators, both of which acted as agents of transfer of resources within British entrepreneurial system. The paradox is that, within colonialism these settled cultivators didn't have the right over means of production and as they were instrumental in marginalizing the practice of shifting cultivation done by the indigene populaceous, they became the unconscious perpetuators of a system of owning land permanently and thereby introducing a compulsive attachment to land, even if it is unproductive. Such new land relations alienated the natives from the collective nature of cultivation by the community and also from collective use of land resulting into the colonial pattern of fragmentation in land that made holding of land meaningless even if it is held by local populace. Further, studies on the nature of indentured labour system pointed out how the planter's control over indentured labourers effected a regime of control over means of production in which mere ownership didn't matter, what mattered is the control over modes of production by way of a structure of contract between factors of production and costs of production. Mostly it was done through control of land and labour, markers of pre-capitalists modes of production brought under Capitalist methods of control through ownership and contract. Similarly, Dasgupta (1983) in her case of study of plantation economy of the Brahmaputra valley examines the capitalistic modes of production in Assam. She notes that the colonial ruler enjoyed a monopoly in the wastelands of the valley through various legislations for leasing and revenue from the land. The colonial ruler imposed heavy taxes to the agricultural lands. These kinds of policies led to the land alienation of tribes like the *Singphos*.

Such regimen of Capitalist mechanisms of control over pre-capitalist modes of production resulted into the disempowerment of ownership of the local community over land and converted this into a source of control over their labouring or productive potential. The capitalist methods were supported by colonial diktats of high taxation and low compensation. One can link this disempowerment of the community through introduction of a concept of ownership with which Alavi (1975) had examined the colonial mode of production in the Indian context that revolved around the question of whether in the last 15 to 20 years there has been a decisive movement in agriculture from a feudal mode of production to a capitalistic mode of production. Alavi points out that the scholars have looked at European (including Russian) historical parallels and theoretical propositions that have been advanced in those contexts but nowhere a reference has been made to the Chinese experience for theoretical contributions.

Alavi suggests that the debate on mode of production should consider the agrarian economy in the wider context of developments in agriculture and the implications arising from these. He argues that concept of feudalism in India neither during the period of direct colonial domination nor during period of 'rural capitalism' can be grasped theoretically except in the context of worldwide structure of imperialism into which it is articulated. He suggests an imperialist mode of production that embraces a global unity as solution to the debate on the mode of production. However, the author notes that this consideration can lead one to a highly problematic area and one may encounter highly theoretical difficulties that cannot be easily solved. Alavi raises a plethora of questions like: would such a unity be premised on a conception of hegemonies or should one assume a hierarchical unity of an imperialist country? Does one recognize disunity and existence of imperialist rivalries? Whatever be the fact he argues that one cannot settle with an already existing definition. At this point one gets a further echo of Sanjib Baruah's paradox. On a global scale, the process of surplus extraction does not allow agrarian production to be autonomous; rather it only contributes to global division of labour and a global mode of surplus extraction. So what does it mean to have a nationalized control over means of production?

Alavi points at the problematic of conceptualization of modes of production because of the *insertion* mode of production into different social formations. Such an insertion is a supportive mechanism of global extraction as it happens in the case of owning the means of production. In this situation, one cannot help but conceptualize the mode of production as part of the whole. The contradictions arising out of conceptualizing these formations as modes of production in the conventional meaning lead one to think about an alternative terminology. On the questions of class alignment he identifies new a class alignment. In this there is new structural dependence between the big Indian bourgeoisie and the imperialist bourgeoisie in the context of changing industrial development. In the post colonial era there is a new basis of subordination of big industrial capital by the metropolitan capital. Within this hierarchical relationship there is convergence of interests between the big Indian bourgeoisie and the imperialist bourgeoisie. This basis is radically different from the subordination of 'comprador' to the imperialist bourgeoisie on the colonial situation when some contradictions between the rising Indian bourgeoisie and the imperialist bourgeoisie came into surface. Alavi feels that it is this, which is central to a consideration of the post-colonial mode of production, and it acts as the basis of the post-colonial State. One could add here that the conflict between the regional and national bourgeoisie over their hold not just over means of production but also more importantly over market does not find a solution in the global circulation of capital. So it enters into the local and regional competition between them to ensure the maximum share of the capital. Are we then to say that the resultant conflict over share of capital in the local and regional is the prime site of development?

Space as a Crucial Marker of Development

As mode of production debate gives us how processes of surplus generation results into a loss of productive capacity and a sharp conflict over who owns how much of capital, it regresses Development to these conflicts. Banerjee-Guha (1992) advocates a new approach to understand process of "development and underdevelopment" in a more holistic way. In fact radical geographers like David Harvey for a very long time has been vigorously nurturing this "new" perspective, which treats the process of accumulation as a profoundly geographical affair. Following the same line of thought, Banerjee-Guha tries to analyze the accumulation in terms of Political Economy of space in general. With the perspective developed from this, she examines the uneven development of colonial India and its spatial continuity, which reflects the present spatial patterns of development in India. What is novel about such an approach is that Space exhibits certain facets of accumulation of surplus in terms of location and its characteristics, which were hitherto not treated as significant. But Space acquires renewed importance as development of productive forces changes the character of geographical and social space radically and by understanding how space had been changed, one understands the effects of development.

The new approach incorporates space into the fold of political economy. It deals the ways in which geographical reordering and restructuring takes place in which spatial strategies and geopolitical elements play key role. Uneven geographical developments present vital aspects of capitalist accumulation and the dynamics of class struggle, both in the past and present, in which means of space act as a crucial determinant of levels of development and its basis in relations of production.

On the basis of this perspective Banerjee-Guha tried to link the uneven development in India and the spatial configuration of the society during the colonial period. The accumulation process carried out by the colonizers through expropriation of surplus gave rise to metropolis cities, which never got deeply integrated into the regional economies and rather acted as 'suction points'. In the eastern region, territorial expansion took the most ruthless form and the excess revenue of this region was used to make up the deficits of the Bombay and the Madras provinces, as this was the principal region where export surpluses originated. With the introduction of plantation cultivation, peasants were separated from their means of production and further the institution of the *Zamindari* system sucked surpluses leading to acute pauperization and extreme poverty. Public investment in irrigation and railways acted as further discriminating factors with the prime motive of irrigation for increasing revenue from agriculture. However with *Ryotwari* and *Mahalwari* agricultural systems in the north, west and the south, lands were given to the people and a direct connection existed between the producer and the State.

The connection and the early subordination of the eastern zone traders and the shrinking of handicraft industry made the region subservient to a settlement system whose locus was in Calcutta. What emerges is a fixed spatial relation between various sectors of production such that agriculture and trading that had a vector of shift away from land to water became the chief medium of merchandise. In another sense spaces were subordinated to give rise to trading and weakening of traditional practices of cultivation and then turning the whole situation subservient to a rent and profit seeking colonial state. This resulted into impoverishment of mass of cultivators and rise of colonial merchandise.

The impact of introduction of colonial relations of production had wide ranging ramifications. Regional identities were fast changing depending upon the role the region played in exchange and accumulation of surpluses, although such identities did not become just economic forces, rather they existed in close relationship with the changes in the economy and spaces like cities. Traditional Indian cities were more inland and related more to internal concerns. These were microcosms of the national, regional or imperial polity. They were made to decline, as they were also the points of resistance to imperialism and were replaced by new port cities. Rising colonial demands also gave rise to a regional specialization and economies of scale that led to the concentration of production in selection of port-cities that became the recipients of migrants and became the centers of collection and consumption.

Changing Relations of Production

What the colonial relations of production resulted in were weakening of traditional base of production and rise of a class of intermediaries who stood to benefit from colonial merchandise. This had exhibited a historical precedent to current weakening of primary sectors of India's development and consequent lopsidedness of development in the economy. Bharadwaj (1982) has made an attempt to understand the persistent slackening of Indian Economy and to explain the factors influencing the process of accumulation, which gives rise to the intricate problem of regional differentiation. Bharadwaj studies the growth pattern of 17 states of India in agriculture and industry with respect to the four periods (1) the colonial period until the world war (2) inter war periods and after, until independence (3) post independence period until the mid sixties (4) period after sixties.

On the basis of secondary data drawn from various sources the author has made insightful observations and generalizations regarding the growth pattern of the states under the study.

According to her, firstly there is an importance of agricultural surpluses in adequate quantity to sustain industrial expansion. The region sharing some industrial vitality appears to be one where agriculture growth has also been promising. For example states like Punjab, Haryana, Gujarat, Maharashtra have always been a high productive region in agricultural sector and they are also simultaneously the most industrialized.

Secondly, public investment appears to have played an important role historically in supporting agricultural growth and in supporting environment for productive channeling of surplus. This is true in the case eastern region of India including the north-eastern part. During the colonial period surpluses extracted from this region by investing in export-based industries such as plantation and oil were used to meet the demand of other provinces. The forced commercialization policies to convert fertile hinterland into provider of cash crops and plantation crops to feed the exports based industries had led to the complete *de-industrialization* in this region. This was coupled with the differential policy of public investment. Public investment in this early colonial period was directed mainly into the railways and irrigation. Bharadwaj's analysis further shows that colonial state not only displaced the traditional modes of production but their method of extraction resulted into stunting any industrial growth.

Thirdly, the regions, which are better off, have utilized the surpluses more productively for forging a link between agriculture and industry. One gets an indication of this when one takes into consideration the per capita level of consumption of the smaller proportion of household that comprises of the lowest bracket of household consumption. In these areas not only the general level of well -being has been relatively higher (for e.g. Gujarat and Haryana) but also a higher industrial activity is observed. It can be interpreted as an association between better agriculture performance and higher level of well-being on one hand and higher industrial performance on the other. But if the region suffers from acute problem poverty it offers breeding grounds of exploitation through usuary, speculative trading, commercial exploitation etc. All these divert surplus from the unproductive channels and create relative advantage of favours to above stated operations the preponderance of such 'unproductive uses' of surplus implies a perverse system of 'social subsidization' that still continues the process of pauperization as the surplus is diverted into unproductive channels.

Formation of Spaces within Nation and the Logic of Capitalist Exchange

Knight (1982) discusses one of the major challenges of the geographers i.e. the present pressure on the fragile world by group territorial identities. Group politico-territorial identities according Knight are not only products of how spaces are organized by the overarching logic of Economic production and exchange, but a riveting of Political interests and territorial affiliations constitutes them. Such a riveting is one of the outcomes of the social processes of which economy plays an important role. But the non-economic component of territorialization assumes importance in Knight's analysis. Giving primacy to the territory, one could put the economic relations differently as a contingently emerged form of exchange relationship that goes along with changes in the conceptualization of the region. With such an open-ended point of view, Knight's *understanding of politico-territorial identity is primarily based on the question of scale and perception.* If territory is regarded as space to which distinct group who holds or covets it attaches identity to that territory and desires to have full control of it for the benefit of the groups. Such a desire for the benefit results into a claim of distinctness. According to Knight there is still a fundamental question that must be answered. Should all groups with distinct territorial and political characteristics have the right to separate territorial and political independence? If the answer is yes, then question arises at what scale? If the answer is no, then should one be content with the status quo or demand through international organization to vouch for the maintenance of the status quo. But desires of the sub national groups for a separate territory have been the dominant trend and have shown no change in the recent past. According to Knight the answer to this dilemma lies in the question as how one defines the "Nation" as a space. At one level of abstraction the Nation is only a conglomerate of regions in the form of extended spatial relations of production that pertains to a definite mode of production and its consequential accumulation.

Dikshit, (1971) makes an attempt to understand the how the nation space is structured within Federalism through the lens of a geographer. He critically analysis the notion of Federalism of earlier geographer as well as social scientists from other disciplines in his quest for a new methodology to understand the geographical underpinning of the concept of Federalism. The author especially critiques Levingstonian notion of Federalism, which is the earliest attempt by a geographer. The author points out that Levingston's analysis is based on a sociological perspective rather than a geographical perspective. He argues that this kind of analysis has failed to yield valuable results in political science as the basic nature of federalism as a polity is based on regionally grouped diversities in a national society. It provides a tool for research, which is not sociological, as it is erroneously thought to be. But Federalism has spatial dimension and as geography deals with spatial interaction, this tool can be used to understand the federal organization of the space of nation-state that purveys a pattern of exchange relation that goes into spatial interaction. Federalism as a political principle organizes and administers space in a manner that there is equilibrium between exchange relation and power relation.

Further, Banerjee-Guha's (2002) paper entitled, "Critical geographical Praxis: Globalization and Socio-Spatial Disorder" concretely characterizes the spatial relations as an order emergent from the extension of the operation of modes of production over space. Such an extension is not an organizational form but it is also a geo-politically determined site of expansion of capital. As Capital flows through spaces like urban-metropolis, it segregates and combines spaces through a logic of reproduction of the relation between market and capital and it gradually usurps the space of labour in the sites of production. Under globalization, such spaces are replicated in order to expand the Capital through a favourable business climate. Such replication and reproduction of spaces acquire a form of cultural landscape as it makes use of local resources and specificity, but creates inherently contradictory relationship between ensuing socio-economic forms, local resources and cultural bases.

It is interesting to trace out how cultural landscapes are reproduced by a certain dominant mode of production that retains and perpetuates existing contradictions between cultural markers and makes use of the contradiction in strengthening the processes of accumulation by a concentration of the means of production among a few classes and individuals. One can surmise that space is produced to serve the material and cultural interests of dominant social groups and such spaces invaginate the non-dominant forms of life in a dialectical relationship such that such forms cannot assert their freedom. The whole politics of the dominant identity and class formation then could be easily managed through a particular spatial formation and the ensemble of relations that it generates. Methodologically such an ordering of the space could be juxtaposed with cultural formations and contestations and such formations in turn would imply a certain form of spatial organization.

Nag, (1993) examines the national formation process of India inflected by a spatial relationship between mainland of India as centre and NEI as periphery, both in cultural and economic senses. The growth of vernacular literature; agitation to a establish particular language as official languages of particular areas; movements of backward nationalities to break away from the advanced nationality in order to earn recognition for themselves were all an internalization of the new post-colonial rights given to every other national identity throughout the country. But such a claim and demand for recognition reinforced the centre-periphery relations when identities of NEI asserted their independence from the mainstream by referring to British days, while in its internal structuring, movement of a particular nationality group evolved an ideology of difference from the parent nationality. The spatial ordering of these movements harped on different living spaces to be demarcated by common national space in terms of distinct cultural markers, while the national market and the national hegemony intended to homogenize and mix them up with each other in order to integrate them with the national mainstream. But internal differentiation, being a cultural and historical fact of life resisted such a process of homogenization, rather the more it was tried, the acute was the resistance resulting into a sub-national consciousness that counterposed the unificatory idea of a common national identity. Taking cues from the Nation's historiography, Nag has explained the multifarious ways of growth of sub-nationalism in India. He argues that in a country where capitalism is slowly reaching new areas and a awakening new cultural groups to life, the streams of sub-nationalist uprisings appears to be unending. The author also argues that the Indian nationality question cannot be studied in exclusion of these aspects because the culmination of this process can alone prove whether India has been a nation-in-the-making or a nation-in-the-unmaking. NEI becomes such a site of making and unmaking of the Nation with waves of subnationalist and ethnic movements.

What emerges from the foregoing discussion is the prevalence of a kind of centre-periphery relationship with the growth of capitalism that orders the social and cultural space in the interest of the Capital. As Capital plays a unificatory role of particular cultural spaces into a homogeneity, it gives rise to its opposite, i.e., forces that perpetuate and sustain difference as reflected in the growing subnationalist movements of NEI. As the process of peripherialization goes unabated so is the process of ordering and reordering of ethnocultural spaces of NEI reflected in the multiplication of nationalities and ethnicities and the expansion of peripheries through each of these claims of distinctness, which simultaneously allows the regime of the Capital by fragmenting the local spaces and gives rise to resistance to capital from multiple sites of national struggle.

On the Development Process in North-East India

Misra (1980), argues that there has been a systematic exploitation of the rich resources of Assam before 1947 by the colonial rulers and since then by the Indian state. She deals extensively the features of this exploitation in the extractive industries of tea, oil and forest. She notes that one positive outcome of the popular movement in the 80s was the emergence of growing awareness of colonial pattern of the exploitation of the Assam's natural resources among the masses. Misra strongly feels that an understanding of colonial pattern of exploitation of Assam's resources can help one to comprehend the more fundamental causes behind the wide by sustained participation of both rural and urban masses in the current movement in the state. In the rural areas the foreign national issue primarily centres around the ownership of the land while the urban centres people saw the problem as one of industrial underdevelopment, a fall out of the colonial pattern, resulting in poverty and large scale unemployment.

She goes in depth of the evolution, functioning and contribution of the extractive industries like tea, oil, and plywood. She comes up with a common pattern of functioning of these industries. According to her, most of these industries extract raw materials from Assam for production and have their marketing units outside the state for which the state is deprived of its revenue earnings. The state has almost a negligible representation in terms of employment in these industries. The Central governments' dualistic policies have marginalized the states of NEI to establish a vibrant economy on the basis of its own rich natural resources.

So, development in the context of NEI, according to Misra would mean a process of larger extraction of resources and its institutionalized ways of draining the economy. What would flow in exchange of such vital resources are residual funds and infrastructure that would be quickly reabsorbed by the same mechanism of drain. She named this vicious cycle as internal colonization of North East India and gave a geographical explanation for continuation for such a process. She demonstrated that as NEI supplies raw and mineral resources. So it acts a hinterland to the economy of the mainland and hence signifies a spatial ordering in which it occupies a place of subordination. In response to such subordination there are popular movements in 80s that attempted to resist this kind internal colonization of NEI.

In another way, how laws of capitalist economy destroys traditional economic bases is studied by Mishra, S.N. (1983). The study traced the dissolution of the tribal economy and the subsequent rise of a new base for the formation of the modern economy. The earlier traditional base of the tribal economy thrived on arrangements like 'Posha' whereby the tribes living in the mountainous track of Arunachal Pradesh had not only the right of levying taxes on the plain's people but also access to material goods as well as services of slaves. The hill tribes in turn guarded the rough terrains from attacks of outsiders. But this traditional economic base started eroding right from the British annexation of Assam. The earlier system of 'Posha' was being monetized and fixed. As a result of this the tribal people lost the right to levy and collect taxes. The outcome of this was that market relations introduced by the colonial state replaced the long lasting dealings between the tribal and plain people. The author notes that the age -old systems survived well after the independence of the country until the Chinese invasion of the region turned the region into a sensitive zone. In fact, the transformation of tribal economy to a new economy after this period through the agency of state has been so dramatic that the author tries to call it a "social revolution" in a Marxian language.

The aforesaid transformation is explained by the author by taking into consideration "the Nishings", one of the hill tribes occupying the lower part of the upper Subanshiri region of Arunachal Pradesh. The first component of the traditional economic basis of the *Nishing* community comprised of such forces of production as land, forest both tropical as well as temperate, hunting and fishing grounds, human population as means of labour and technical knowledge in tools made from metals were used for various purposes. The second component of the economic basis comprised of the relations of production including those of distribution, circulation and exchange of products. In the traditional economy of the *Nishings*, the surplus produce is bartered for necessities like clothing, metal goods, pots and salt and finally for an animal called *mithun*. Families in deficit borrow from those who have surplus and return the borrowed amount in the next harvest or even later. There was no concept of interest or capital.

According to Mishra, the production process which consists of sequential or simultaneous sub-processes like those of slashing the vegetation cover, burning the debris, sowing seed, fencing, harvesting etc. itself rest or subsume two sets of relations (1) the relations among the workers deployed for carrying out the production processes including the norms of labour cooperation, and (2) the relations of workers with means of production, namely land and instruments of labour. Both these sets of relations among *Nishings* were based on customary institutions enjoying community sanctions.

After 1960 all the tribes of the Arunachal Pradesh came under the scope of the state sponsored development. The state through various schemes and subsidies vigorously campaigned for the permanent settlement and subsequently the *jhum* fields were converted into orchards or developed for permanent irrigated cultivation. The story sounds similar to the processes of settled cultivation that disempowered other traditional communities of NEI from choosing a suitable range of optimum productive methods and means. So, formation of state property has been partly at the cost of the common property. As a result the old relations of production have been in the process of breaking down. Along with the private relations, market and money have taken root. In the new economic environment money acquired a store value and became a means of private accumulation. Unlike the traditional system, labour is being commercialized in the new economic set up. Finally, with private property formation in land and other assets, with increasing role of money in production relations and accumulation of money capital, there has been increase in differentiation in income and consumption of the families belonging to a tribe.

In the case of Arunachal Pradesh this transformations from dissolution of the traditional base of the economy to formations of the modern base of the economy the only external force is the State. However this has not been the case of some other states of northeast where beside the state other external factors e.g. immigration from neighboring regions have also influenced this transformation.

In similar vein D.K. Misra's (2001) paper documents all the changes and analyses some aspects of these process of change, focusing on interplay of three distinct forces: the market, the state and the community in the case of Arunachal Pradesh. In the post independence period, the people of the state have experienced enormous changes at different levels. In the structural transformation of the Arunachal's economy the decline is manifested in the expansion of productive capacity of the economy, the decline in the relative importance of primary sector, occupational diversification of the work force, increasing marketization and monetization of the exchange process and changes in property rights.

Mishra begins his paper with the influence of the of the twin agents of the market and state on the transformations of tribal social formations and presents the case of agriculture and forest related activities and he finally concludes the paper with implications of these changes and the role played by the forces of the state, market and community.

The author notes that the two process of change - the internal forces, which arises itself from the indigenous tribal social formations and external forces mainly the state and the market. It is the interplay of these two forces, which has led to the transformations in the political economy of the agrarian structure. In the case of Arunachal Pradesh, the State underwent epochal changes during the colonial era. During this period, the traditional tribal economy got dissolved. The twin agents of market and state in the modern time have transformed tremendously the tribal social formations, especially the agriculture. In fact state has predominance over market as the principal modernizing agent, which has created a process of transition in Arunachal Pradesh that has its own specificities.

The major change that the author notes with regard to the state's agrarian scene is the change in the cropping pattern, contribution of agriculture to the economy etc. The state has witnessed high proportion of commercial cultivation and agricultural labourers, a change in the cropping pattern with a high percentage of increase in non food grains at the cost of the food grains, a shift towards private and individual ownership of holding and a shift of manpower to the non-farm sector.

With mutually reinforcing role of population growth, the market and the state, the nature of ownership of rights over land and forests has changed. The encouragement for switching over from shifting cultivation to permanent cultivation, land improvement grants, incentives for plantation of cash crops and even training to individual farmers to acquire skills led to formation of private property rights. Increasing penetration of capitalism has transformed the notion of property rights also.

On one hand the emergence of new elite, the shift of manpower from rural to urban occupations, linking of villages from interior areas to areas with better communications have undermined the effective authority of traditional institutions. On the other hand, electoral democracy and development projects have opened up new areas to exercise control over it. The immigration of large number of outsiders to the state, particularly to the areas as agricultural laborers and tenants has also forced the local communities to rethink their rules for providing access to resources.

But how this transformation affects the construction of agency of the tribal identity has been highlighted by Roy Burman (1989) and on the basis of this conceptualization of agency of the tribal, he discussed what are the constraints to their development, both internal and external.

According to the author the tribe as a social formation may be identified in two ways – first as a stage in the history of evolution of societies and second, as a society organized on the basis of kinship ties which enables it to be a multifunctional grouping. On this basis, he argues that a tribe can outgrow its primitiveness and retain the social boundary, which is an essential feature of its identity.

The author distinguishes proto-nationalism and infra nationalism from sub-nationalism. According to him in the first two phases of the identity expansion of ethnic groups, the group remained isolated from the dominant political mobilization leading to state formation. This isolation continued as long as the tribal base of the economy could withstand the onslaught of modern capitalist economy. This withstanding was possible by the cultural synergy between tribal mores and system of production. Contrastingly, Sub-nationalism is a phase of contraction of ethnic identities which got closely involved in the dominant process of the state but among which parochial loyalties are coming forth as an outcome of inquitous functioning of the state apparatus.

With this conceptual framework, when the tribal situation in the North-East India (NEI) is examined with respect to the constraints in the development of protonational process, it could be found that the tribal entities get oriented to the statist processes of India, which comes out in sharp focus. The first is the historical memory of the tribes and the hiatus in the perception of the meaning of historical events among the tribals and the non-tribals. Second is the effective cognitive difference about the cultural rights and the structures and strategies of resource mobilizations.

The author argues that looking at the strategic location of NEI, policy planners should have the sensitivity and awareness in the happenings of neighboring countries of the sub continents of Asia. It is further argued that in the NEI tribal communities tend to constitute marginalized status class. National unity in NEI can be cemented only by encompassing the significance of India as the vanguard nation against colonialism and as one committed to non-capitalist path of development. However, a consistent and continuous manifestation of these ideological dimensions must be there in addition to emotional and material dimension.

The author critiques the development strategy put forward by the center. He argues that in terms of political economy "anti development" is taking place through development policies. The land reform policies that envisages abolition of exploitative intermediaries between the state and the individual has serious constraints in tribal economies of NEI, as tribal communities derive only a part of the food products such as roots, tubers, and leaves and other jungle products that are collected by the communities. Hence, the implementation of such policies is considered to actually dispose the tribal households from community-based resources. Policies such as the recommendation of the National Committee on Development of Backward areas for the individualization of communal ownership of land will in fact lead to neo-federal rights.

In similar light Acharya (1998) made an attempt to study the some of the ethnic process in the NEI. The author draws the theoretical framework heavily from the analytical models in Soviet ethnography, particularly the works of Yulian Broomley. However to explain the ethnic complexities in India with its unique caste system and strong popular feelings about Indian "nation" he introduces certain other concepts and terms. His paper begins with an introduction of ethnos and ethnics, which are highly misused in the literature of social anthropology. The second half of the paper mainly discusses the ethnic processes such as –ethnic divergence, ethnogenic interethnic consolidation, ethnogenic mixing, inter ethnic consolidation and finally the process of assimilation. While dealing with these processes the author reviews the earlier works and discusses them in an elaborative manner with respect to the present situation. The paper examines the complex pattern of these aforesaid ethnic processes with reference to India in general and NEI in particular.

Can such suggestions about reorientation of paths of development and reempowerment of tribals through a process of ethnogenesis in NEI alter the process of marginalization and peripherialization?

Political Structures and Development in Northeast India

Sanjib Baruah (1989) analyses the pros and cons of the minority policy advocated by the Centre and its future ramifications. He opines that the present minority policy of the Centre is in fact a continuation of the British policy that aimed at the protection of the vulnerable indigenous people. The author argues that the minority policy advocated for NEI in one hand has witnessed certain achievements it has posed serious dangers in an ethnically majority region like and the North East.

The present policy, which emphasizes the protection of the vulnerable indigenous people from their more crafty neighbours is a reluctant continuation even though it is out of favor to Indian national circles. The Britishers during the Colonial days carried exclusive protectionist policies e.g. the "Inner Line Policy" by which the area beyond the line was left to the indigenous people to manage their own affairs. Although colonial administration cited the importance of preserving ethnic communities from outsiders but the major reason behind not extending the British administration to these areas was the political risks and financial expenses involved in it.

One gets the reflection of the effect of this type of policies among the tribal leaders in states like Arunachal Pradesh, Nagaland and Mizoram. The idea is to follow a path of self-development without the distortions from the external factors. Therefore during the popular agitation against the immigrants in Assam in the 80s there was a demand for the extension of the Inner Line to Assam in order to protect the ethnic minorities. But such insularity from the outside world not only distanced them from the mainstream, but also stopped their coming out from their own habitats. It strongly created a self-consciousness that did not allow any space to the other, while this space of self-consciousness; indeed its very assertion signified an ongoing intrusion or affectation of tribal suzerainty by external forces. In all senses this was a reaction of the tribal communities to external threats, but such a reaction could not stop the way such forces impeded the path of self-development.

A second element of this policy according to Baruah, is the diffusion of a model of political autonomy through culturally defined states that was mainly developed with respect to peninsular India. However, there are certain benefits and dangers of such policies. The notion of legitimized demand on the basis of language has a different connotation in an ethnically diverse region like NEI, where there is no single dominance of language, which acted as a divisive factor. Unlike in the Indian mainland, where political movements demanded separate statehood on the basis common language, in Northeast India such movements based their mobilization mostly on symbols other than these languages. The demand for Hill state in various parts of northeast India attempted to mobilize the sentiments of the hill people against the plainsman. What eventually emerged, as a result of this kind of demands was not a single hill state but a number of mini states.

The author identifies the benefits of such statehood whereby the mini states have been allowed to elect the representatives of the indigenous people to gain power at the state level and to determine policy in areas that are the under the constitutional jurisdiction of states. He also feels that political, social and economic consequences of the policies carried out by the elected governments were drastic in which the indigenous people enjoy majority status. In state like Mizoram and Arunachal Pradesh where the legislature is dominated by representatives of the indigenous people it has extended and strengthened policies of protective discrimination in favor of schedule tribes in govt. employment, allocation of govt. contracts, transfer of land and property to non-tribal been made extensively difficult.

He concludes with a view that the assumption that there are exclusive groups that can be given statehood or autonomy in their territories is predominantly problematic in the context of NEI. To impose such a model there is to court danger of inter-ethnic strife, despite its effectiveness so far.

Mukhopadhay (1998) identifies the factors of under development of the state of Arunachal Pradesh and manifestations of these on the state. Arunachal Pradesh is endowed with good hydroelectric potential, rich in mineral and forest resources but due to certain drawbacks, the development of the State has been hampered. She points out that most of the investment is exploitative in nature, mainly involved in the extraction of the rich forest wealth. There has been ruthless cutting of the medicinal plants by new drug companies on which the tribal people heavily depend for medical cure. Various government plans have been implemented and some are in the pipeline but most of them have been ineffective and the institutions set up for the implementation have turned out to be a white elephant. According to the author, basic problem is the failure to identify the factors which have alienated the people in Arunachal Pradesh from the rest of the country. Other factors like erratic power supply, intermittent floods, poor roads, lack of entrepreneurial culture and persistent militancy have slowed the development process of the region. She argues that there has been a superimposition of mainstream political structures over the region's traditional autonomous socio-political institutions and the Indian State has not focused on the development of tribal culture but imposed mainstream cultural hegemony. The emergences of new educated groups have found that their traditional ways of living are being threatened by the forces of modernization. A movement for the resurrection of indigenous identity has been started by the intellectuals of the state to mobilize the mass. She criticizes the Central government for its inability to comprehend the intricacies of such development and its lapses to address the socio-economic problem.

Sinha (1998) draws an understanding of the NEI as a territorial entity and its relationship with the Indian State with the help of the politico-cybernetic models of the State. One of the models presumes the 'state' to be a unicellular organism with nuclei (centre, core, and capital). It also considers a system in which continuous surveillance by the dominant forces on the subordinates' behaviour and deployment of threats and punishments are normal ingredients. All these are performed in terms of power, which is defined as control over communication flows, located in the state at one point where decisions are made and information is transmitted. In such a politico-cybernetic model of the state, the extensive territorial entity such as India according to Sinha is nothing but a hierarchy of power centres upwardly branching out to a seat of ultimate decision-making power. In such a model the commands follow down from the centre to the periphery and information travel in the reverse direction. In the normative model the state, power is replaced by the concept of collective consensus on shared norms and values. Here the emphasis is placed on society, considered to be a commonality of immaterial elements such as images and moral codes. Status and prestige are peacefully and unanimously accorded to those who fill the most strategic roles in the societies. It is presumed there exists a central zone in the realm of the values, beliefs and actions in the structure of society. This central zone also provides a set of activities, roles and personnel within the network of institutions. In this way the central zone is intimately connected with society considered to be sacred and ideal as espoused by the ruling authority. From this point of view, India as a territorial entity has a number of sub-systems, such as polity, economy, status, ecclesiastical and kinship systems etc. which are organized through common and overlapping sets of values and personnel. These types of sub-subsystems characterize the pattern of authority symbolized by individual behaviour.

In this context Sinha finds a closer empirical reality of inter-relationship between the Indian mainstream (or the core) and the North-Eastern frontiers. These frontier states are tenuously linked with the Centre, where the strategic elite are located, significant decisions are made, commands are transmitted to the peripheries and the information are demanded from them. The key terms, which qualify the relationship between the two, are power, legitimacy, authority, rule and compliance. Sinha points out that such relations are formal, mechanical and legal that sprang up because of some historical accident but is sought to be given paramount importance. The pattern of this relationship smacks of colonial attitude of the past, to which the new rulers have added a paternalistic veneer of development and planning for the backward region.

Such a relationship emerges in a particular pattern in the grassroot institutions of development as well. Duggal Verma and Mathew (1999) in their studies of nature of governance in the state of Nagaland points out the two contradictions –the micro-micro and the macro-micro. In the former case the traditional Village Council (VC) has failed to check the corruption within the Village Development Council (VDB) created by the state under the VC to initiate development programs. The study finds that in the traditional matter the VC functions smoothly and in the case of VDB, the VC has failed to assert its authority and check corruption (micro-micro). The same contradiction is also observed when indigenous people are put in the higher hierarchy of decision making (the state, the districts) and a body to carry out the development programme under it the same problem persists (macro-micro). There has been large elite appropriation of the public and leakages in the development funds.

Agrarian base of the Economy and Politics of Development

Karna (1990) deals with the changes with respect to the agrarian scenario of NEI and notes that there has been an increasing shift towards commercialization of tillage practices and nature and extent of labour uses. Drawing from various micro studies of the hills of Meghalaya, Mizoram, Tripura, Manipur he points that the jhumias of NEI region are now cultivating cash crops increasingly. Under such a market system there is a monopoly of a trading and merchant classes mostly from outside the region. In case of Meghalaya and Mizoram he notes that cash crops cultivation is becoming popular where an easy produce has a quick market enabling higher returns. This transformation not only brought the tribal land to the market but also the possibility to buy tribal labour. Under the influence of linkages outside, the tribal people are renting out land to new immigrant sharecroppers from whom they never have been able to recover the land and thus losing away the vital means of production.

Another significant depletion of traditional practices of cultivation lay in depriving the tribal communities from their traditional community landholding by way of discouraging the practice of 'shifting cultivation' by the State. Such a discouragement not only alienated the tribals from the community based forest farming but also consequent degradation of the soil quality. The development policies pursued by various governments resulted into shrinking of *Jhum* cropping area and as a result created wasteland. Choudhury (1998) demonstrated that replacement of *Jhum* by settled cultivation brought in the necessity of aforestation and wasteland development. But such programmes reverse the historically naturalized relationship between forestland and agricultural land, which hitherto established a kind of harmony between agricultural productivity and forest cover. The breach in this relationship not only unsettled the traditional ways of natural resource management but it had resulted into a prima facie degradation of land, to be later rejuvenated by using permanent plantation and introduction of sedentary agricultural activities. This is not only an imposition on the traditional resource management but a depletion of the resource base itself. It demonstrates a high degree of insensitivity and pursuance of counter productive developmental programmes.

What emerges is the concrete evidence of the damage done by introduction of commercialized idea of agriculture and land use through the developmental plans that aim at changing the production relations with its worsening effects on the region. Such adverse effects are compounded in the rise of private property in every sphere of life that results into further misery and deprivation to the tribes of NEI.

A Holistic Counterhegemonic Framework of Struggle for Development

Biswas (1997) and Biswas and Suklabaidya (forthcoming, 2003) argues that it is the nature of cultural politics in North East India that decides even the mode of production explanation of development in the holistic sense. They identify cultural politics as a Politics of responsibility that expresses the extent to which ethnic communities of the NEI region launch struggles against dominance. The experience of being dominated goes with the lived experience of marginalization in every sphere of life and hence resulted into making of counter hegemonic struggles. The impetus for such counter hegemonic struggle lies in the perception that a periphery like NEI always has the real danger of being subdued in the process of Development as the national framework of development always gives rise to alienation from traditional practices and more drastically a class of neo-elites who directly serve the interest of National Capital and who manipulate and distort the development process in favour of forces that displace the internal sources of development, be it resources or local knowledge. They consider this process of domination through development as one of plank of carrying out popular democratic politics and forces within NEI tacitly fall to a collaborator of this. Yet there are radicals and the mundane who together in their own ways subvert the almost colonial structure of development packages even at the cost of underdevelopment. In other words, modes of development alien to the cultural politics of North East need to overcome this ground level resistance from already existing social formations. Ignoring these formations for the sake of National development is an anathema.

So the all-important questions are two: how do the developmental policies of the State strengthen/weaken the resource base and production relation that already exists in NEI? Next, how does the exchange relationship give rise to the dominant form of economic relations that marginalized the non-economic forces of production? Answer to these questions involves the underpinnings of social and political constructions of identities that appear through binary oppositions between dominance and counter-dominance, the cultural and the economic etc. clearly showing a relative autonomy of functioning of identities. Such functions produce new relationships in interrelated domains of social life. Developmental process in NEI, therefore, involves crucial variables like cultural articulations of identities and economically determined processes of production and reproduction.

The Problem

On the developmental debate (Griffin, 1968; Frank, 1969) investigations in political economy consists in isolating the specific modes and the relationship of dominance and dependency that exists at various points in the socio-historico and cultural processes. In the case of North-East India (NEI) it can be imbricated within a metropolitan-satellite relationships that subsists *in* the Indian Capital and the Indian State. Evidence for this lies at the unequal exchange of resources and products, flights of capital from NEI, increasing pressure on the fixed factors of production like land etc. All these find its reflection in the state of the economy of the NEI, which by all parameters turn out to be underdeveloped in comparison to the national scenario.

To understand the nature and causes of underdevelopment in NEI, this essay tentatively explores the linkages between the modes of development and the modes of production in order to arrive at a global explanation to the phenomena of underdevelopment. The essay considers the following vital questions-

What is the nature of accumulation and its impact on the modes of production prevalent in NEI?

In what way the Indian State operate at the local and the regional levels? Does it conform/contradict to this process of dependent accumulation?

What are the structural components of dependency relationships, especially the matrix of social relationship that sustains dependency?

How are the positive indexes of the underdevelopment, which are levels attained in the operation of a certain modes of development related to modes of production?

What are the political and cultural expressions of underdevelopment in the specific context of NEI?

Selection of these problems centre around an explanation of two interdependent yet distinguishing phenomenon of political economy and cultural identity (ies) without reducing one to the other. Such an explanation would bring together political economy and culture close to each other and bridge some distance between them while they cannot be reduced to just components of a singular explanation. This could be understood by referring to relative autonomy of the superstructure, which would act as a guiding point to disseminate these specificities of devėlopment in NEI.

Given this irreducibility of Culture into Economics and vice-versa the question is, how does one go about explaining the fact of resistance to the dominant discourse of development that centres around dominant mode of production? The dominant discourse of development in all possible ways indicates to a top-down process than a bottom up approach to the question of empowerment of NEI in seeking solutions that are derived from the self-defined positionality of a periphery. How does one understand the self-defined cultural, political and economic positionalities of a number of ethnic and student organizations of NEI? Is it that Economic demands, as understood by a section of scholars on North- East India given the least priority on the agenda of social movements from NEI? Is it true that such movements are merely ethnocentric without sharing anything in common with the mainstream? Or, what are the ways in which a substantive give and take is possible between North- East and India?

The stereotype of NEI being isolated from national mainstream produce a significant cognitive distortion in understanding the possibilities of conflict resolution at least at the level of sharing certain common goals of development. The incommensurability of goals notwithstanding what middle grounds could be explored in ensuring a lasting peace in the conflict-ridden region of NEI is a question mark still.

Approach to the Problem

The study takes into account the limitations of fragmented, isolated and piecemeal nature of empirical enquiries into the development of North-East India (NEI), which are limited to explaining 'what happens when' kinds of situations. A large number of scholars of NEI, therefore presents the dilemma over combining the empirical and normative. But the prevailing social and political scenario of NEI presents a complex picture of political mobilization that bases itself on the indexes of social and economic development. The situation throws up the challenge to investigate into the causal and historical linkages between politics and economics, which in turn compel most of the scholars to evolve a quasi-political explanation of social and economic development. Given this situational compulsions one has to find out broad enough categories of development in order to accomplish the task of understanding and situating development in an integrative perspectives of politics and economics.

Keeping this in mind the primary question to approach the problem of this essay is how to relate modes of development with the modes of production. As there are no clear distinguishable characteristics of modes of development with respect to the modes of production, one needs to develop a staged connection between the two.

The central premise for understanding development is that actors and agencies are structurally determined to engage within the given modes of production which came into being due to a number of historical, social and cultural factors. In the case of North-East India such factors of historical importance are often political and cultural that act as 'response factors'. In other words, they assume an apriori role over economic development. To put it in more firmly, no development in North-East India is bereft of a distinct political and cultural mobilization and it is in this sense that development assumes a political economy phenomenon with its cultural implications.

To begin with one could look into the internal and external relationships between labour processes and commodification within particular mode of production. How modes of development are related to modes of production could be understood in terms of identifying actual and possible shifts in crucial indicators of development that reflects the relationship between the labour process and commodification.

An economy, largely dominated by the primary sector, the dominant labour processes in agricultural production is 'domestic', as it primarily serves the consumption needs of the family and the community with a negligible surplus for market. The relationship between dominant labour processes and commodification is weak within domestic modes of production, as it does not allow enough marketable surplus. This point could be properly corroborated by taking into account data from ethnographic and anthropological studies of '*jhum*' cultivation and communal sharing of cultivable land. It could be further elicited by taking into account the nature of monetary transactions, investments and consumption pattern in sample villages from representative states of the region.

Along with the domestic modes of production there is coexistence of forms of capitalistic modes of production like a hybrid mix of externally dependent monopolists, individual intermediaries in the manufacturing sectors and the service sector composed of totally dependent service class, contractors, dealers, merchants and others. Three basic activities seem to be determined in this modes of production, namely production, mediation of exchanges and consumption with respect to which sub-modes could be delineated: formation of regional Capital, intermediaries and dependents. These modes of production taken as a whole do not assume uniformity across various side sectors of production, rather one can identify a difference between a manufacturer and a dealer and a consumer, all tied by a common thread of larger dependence of this mode on the national and international market. Even among the manufacturers some are monopolist especially in oil and tea industries while others are a subsidiary of giant manufacturing industries outside the region. Among the dealers some enjoy the privilege of strong linkage with national market for which most are merchants from out-side the region. The consumer class is again sharply divided in terms of their accessibility to market while they are dependent on the spin-offs from the market. An increasingly capitalistic mode of production produces more and more dependency among classes of producer, dealer and consumer.

An analysis of this variation within capitalistic modes of production would be carried out in terms of other relations with the external market. Internally these strata of producer, dealer and consumer present another picture of dependence as they are polarized in relation to each others access to the market.

The question is, given two broad modes of production, one peripheral modes of production and another dependent capitalistic modes of production, *what are the possible modes of development*? One can understand the possible modes of development in terms of the nature of accumulation. As domestic and dependent capitalistic mode of production together gives rise to expropriation of surplus without an equivalent appropriation, the situation leads to a stagnation and underdevelopment with the feature of an internal colony and an absence of appropriate technology and strategies of Development (Butola 1996, Misra 2000, Miri 1996,2003). The possibilities of development are constrained by the structural domination of national Capital over the regional capital, lack of extended reproduction of labour processes and distributive asymmetries between components of various modes of production. All these together compound the ambiguity of maintaining a culture specific lifestyle and slips into the dominant discourse of adopting what the State or any other agency of the Pan-Indian ruling class decides to bring forth in the name of development showing a very limited role of choices that emanate from communities of NEI.

Table No. 1
Interrelationship between Modes of Development and Modes of Production

Modes of Production	Domestic	Intermediary	Capitalist
Modes of Development	Self-reliant	Development of Local Markets	Dependent
Accumulation	Primitive Accumulation	Marketable Surplus	Expropriation without Appropriation
Institutions	Local and Communitarian	Trading & Business Agencies, Local Corporate Bodies	Industrial sector Financial Institutions Service and Welfare Sector
Classes	Rural Petty Bourgeoisie	Regional Petty Bourgeoisie	Middle Class & Regional Bourgeoisie

Identification of such factors would lead us to understand the roles of various actors and agencies in the process of development. As modes of production equals the combinations of social relations of production and the levels of development of productive forces, the approach presents the possibility of distinguishing the agency from the structure. Therefore the task is to identify agency both in the State as well as in the productive classes in order to bring out the social relations of production in terms of which development could be characterized. Following this, a tentative model of interrelationships between modes of development and modes of production in the context of North–East India could be present like above.

In the table above, interrelationship between modes of production and modes of development, the nature of accumulation, institutional networks and classes are taken as the manifest of outcome of modes of production modes of development. If modes of development are derived from modes of production a structural relationship could be established between economy and processes of development which involves an ensemble of institutional, political and economic relations. The ensemble could be understood only if there is a structural relationship between modes of development and modes of production. The structural relationship between modes of production and modes of development could be understood from the premise that development is development of productive forces qua modes of production. Further, one can conceive development as a process of internal growth with specific reference to a society or a culture only if ensemble of social relations is structurally reproduced. This structural reproduction of the ensemble of social relations is a part of the relations of reproduction that emanates from particular modes of production. In other words, the autonomy of development has relations of reproduction that could be understood from how modes of production determine a particular form of reproduction which, becomes a part of universal and generalized reproduction of an ensemble of production relations. Development assumes autonomy within the structural relations of production by way of changing and modifying the relations of reproduction. Strategies of development aim at altering and restructuring these relations of reproduction, which are the outcome of the ensemble of production relations. Given such a structural relationship between modes of production and modes of development one can conceptualize the relationship in the context of NEI.

As the table shows domestic and peripheral modes of production gives rise to a self-reliant mode of development in the sense that this particular mode of production aims at self-fulfilling consumption at the individual and community level typically available in the peripheral locations of NEI. These peripheral locations assume the form of 'self-enclosed little economies' in which production and reproduction follow a harmonious pattern. Similarly, in the Intermediary modes of production there is production of surplus through mercantile activities that is continued and sustained through relations of unequal exchange. But such relations of unequal exchange cannot take the form of extended reproduction of marketable surplus as it cannot enhance the productive capacity. There is only a horizontal extension of the market limited by the extent to which exchange relations establishes a balance between trading and surplus. In other words, market relations do not assume an autonomy over and above what is produced by a given modes of production. In this intermediary modes of production, development assume an in-egalitarian form of give and take where the redistribution is constrained by the calculus of gains and losses. In the context of NEI to the most happening layer of the society lies at this intermediary modes of production as it represents the exchange potential of communities. Further, to this the capitalist modes of production centred on maximization of profit assume an outward orientation whereby the products from industries are sold in the market lying outside the region. This mode of production manifests the dualism of internal and external markets at movements of goods and services. As the sector depends heavily on profits from such unequal exchange giving in to the external market it results in accumulation of surplus conditioned by demands outside. Such dependency relations bring in subordination of the local capitalist by the larger core of Indian economy, which restricts their developmental potentialities.

As part of the structural relations between modes of production and modes of development, the nature of accumulation presents how capital is circulated within a mode of production. The classical notion of primitive accumulation in the form of owning and expanding private property gets metamorphosed into development of sustainable homestead economy thriving upon an emphasis on stock of produce meant for future consumption. Such stockpiling of produce is balanced by an assessment of the collective vis-à-vis individual, household necessity. Such an accumulation does not flow into circulation of commodities, rather it grows limit upon the possibilities of uncontrolled accumulation. In the case of NEI such accumulation could be conceived as non-capitalist modes of production, which does not only resist commodification but also arrests unequal exchange. Although such a mode of production does not enhance productive forces, it retains a horizontal equality of exchanges outside commodification. By remaining outside the sphere of commodification, domestic mode of production becomes the basis for community based resource management.

As the Capitalist processes of uneven development simultaneously includes and excludes the primary modes of production, primitive accumulation in domestic and peripheral modes of production exists as a source of alterity and difference. Such a difference assumes an autonomous space which is strikingly present in the hill economies of NEI. The uneven linkages that such a sector develops with the intermediary and the capitalist modes of production results into coexistence of mutually exclusive modes of production. This presents inherently contradictory layers of modes of production and positions the weaker amongst the stronger, thereby giving rise to the rule of the capitalist relations of production over primary modes or production. Development strategies aim at producing a minimum balance or a reflective equilibrium between these mutually exclusive modes of production, each of which give rise to a corresponding mode of development. The primary question before the development theories would be, does the coexistence of the contradictory modes of production make development limited by the structure? One way to answer the question is to maintain that development being the central metaphor of capitalist modes of production yields to heterogeneous social forms that constitute a coexistence of contradictory modes of production. Therefore, what comes after development of capitalist modes of production is this coexistence of primary, intermediary and capitalist modes of production within which the substitution of the weaker the by the dominant results into a displacement of heterogeneity. In another way, to answer the question could be to search out the conditions of the coexistence of contradictory modes of production sustained by a hierarchy of structural relations that include the ensemble of social relations and patterns of accumulation. In both the ways, neither the substituting of the weaker by the dominant nor the perpetuation of the hierarchy of contradictory modes of production clear out the space for development. Rather it creates gaps and fissure within development relegating a certain strata to the weaker mode of production while erecting another strata of the dominant. Therefore, the weaker and the dominant mutually constitute each other as something simultaneously contradictory and yet coexisting, continuously generating a force of displacement and heterogeneity through a hierarchical ordering. Within this hierarchy the weaker modes of production constitute the dominant via its annihilation through development, while the stronger constitutes the weaker via underdevelopment. While development tries to appropriate underdevelopment in the forms of capitalist modes of production appropriating the labour processes of other weaker modes of production, it appropriates a part of the weaker through development, while it leaves aside another part as underdevelopment lying at the margins of capitalist economy. This process of development of underdevelopment goes along with transformation of capitalist accumulation from local to the global. This is a kind of upward displacement from the local into the global which implies a displacement of periphery into centre. The development process in the context of NEI bears these contours of development of underdevelopment in the relationship between coexisting modes of production that acts in a contradictory manner to displace and replace indigenous modes of production (mostly domestic and peripheral) into capitalist modes of production.

Methodology

The problematique of understanding the complex relationship between the modes of production and modes of development and its cultural implications calls for a critique of development and various alternatives that follow from such a critique. The critiques need to move from commonsense to critical sense, as it has to address not only the systemic factors of development but also the local and micro level responses to what come form above. The standard political economy method that makes use of modes of production argument give an inkling into structural relations of production and reproduction both at the material and cultural levels. So, the essay has to draw an equation between political economy and culture but such an equation is not possible without taking into account the concrete situation of NEI. The concrete situation involves the emergence of ethnic movements and spacing of such movements, exhibiting the production of political identities in space and time. But space and time are not givens rather they are socially and culturally constructed as an affect of economic reationality and political imagination. The claim of being a tribal or a member of an ethnic community gives rise to complex process of spacing the self in the horizon of history. Further, history assumes the form of relations of material production and what follows from such relations. In the practice of spacing the self-identity the NEI communities appropriate a certain relation between time and production and inscribes an identity on such abstract markers of engagements with nature and culture. Within this engagement there is an underdetermination of political and cultural identities by the lived experience of tribes and communities that primarily centers around their rule in socially productive domains of Economy. The all-important questions become how does one space oneself in the Space produced by concrete political economy? Is there a political economy of production of space that determines the claims of engagement?

One has to establish a relationship between political economy, culture and space as triple registers of development and construction of social identities in the context of NEI. Space provides the necessary context to apply development as a category, which has its central implication in the production of cultural identity. But space cannot be understood without taking into account the political economy of production of space itself, which moves from organization and production in space to production of space that mediates relations of production.

To understand how these mediations take place one has to look into the space of representation in which modes of production signify a certain mode of development. So, the question is how the space of representation is constituted? To answer this how question one has to look into the 'what' question as the constitutions of space shows a certain mode of being i.e. conditions of existence. These conditions of existence are manifested in the inalienable relations between being and having, having and becoming, which are both related to the space of production in which the economy functions to fulfill the conditions of existence that are ontological to the mode of being. Modes of being as constituent of the space are synthesis between production and conditions of existence. Therefore, to understand the space of representation one needs to interpret how economy functions through various modes of production that give rise to the relationship between preduction and the space of self-identity. Such an interpretation has to take into account the production of surplus and the linkage with historical development of modes of production that go into definition of the space for one's self –identity. So, one has to follow a hermeneutic method that combines both political economy and cultural identity through the space of representation,

But the space of representation is an abstract, heterogeneous, contradictory and emergent space. Such an uneven nature of space is simultaneously transcendental and experiential. It is transcendental in the sense that it is the condition of the possibility of situating ones knowledge of oneself, while it is experiential in the form of the inalienable grounding of the subjective, objective and inter- subjective dimensions of ones ties with a particular history and a particular culture. There is often a possibility of cognitive plurality based upon the positioning of the human subject. The way one projects a self conscious understanding of ones relationship with the world gives one the fundamental basis for reproducing one's self in the concrete social relations of production, while such relations manifest themselves in an external objective space of existence produced by activity of production. But the space produced by the activity of production remains external to the space of consciousness. Phenomenologically speaking such an external relations between the produced space and the space of consciousness, operates in any space of representation and determines the form of cultural, ethnic or political identity. Further exploring this space of representation as a byproduct of the relation between the socially produced space and the space of consciousness, one would perceive dialectic between the two. In a situation of multiple modes of production within the social formations of NEI it is the dialectic between the capitalist relations of production and its others is what determines the space of representation. The space of representation envelops the contradiction between the modes of production as well as limiting the conditions that arise from this contradiction. The limit imposed by the contradiction between the modes of production in turn limits the space of representation. Such a limitation of the space of representation acts as a constraint in our understanding of space of representation, which could be overcome if one can identify a ser of critical praxis that explains how the space mediates various essential factions of the economy.

The meditative role of the space is simultaneously spatial and conceptual. The spatial aspects could be retrieved by following the geography of knowledge in relation to production of identity and their embeddedness in relations of production. The primary question of is this mode of enquiry is a methodological one: can we have a spatial reference to distinct modes of production that embed inalienable social and political identity? One would suggest a critical geographical practice of disclosing the nature of space as the determinant of the claims of identity. This is possible by way of locating the sites of economic production in relation to non-economic conditions of production. Such a relationship takes a leaf from the naturalized pre-given mode of production to a critique of production that opens up how the activity of capital and surplus generate a particular kind of development, i.e. a leap from political economy to the sphere of development that involves a number of non-economic factors. Such non-economic factors manifest themselves in space as a form of unaccounted surplus, which is beyond a surplus generating economy, an extension of production relation beyond the site of production and market. Such an extension overhauls the space of production into the nature of reproduction that flows into in-between spaces between production and surplus. These in-between-spaces operate beyond capital as it originates from the relations of reproduction and moves into the development of non-capitalist-non-economic zones of social relations. This extended form of production of social identities that incorporates naturalized space of production and moves beyond it combines the transient and the experiential aspects of Space and overcomes the limit of structural relations of production. This shows up the newer possibility of a critical geography of identity in emergent spaces that gives a new meaning of development and shifts the paradigms from the production of space to spacing of identities in hitherto unfamiliar spaces.

Finally, to avoid the dichotomy between the a top-down and a bottom-up approach one has to leave open a formulation of modes of development to an interface between contemporary politics and social movements which would keep the conclusion open ended.

2

Political Economy of Under-development of N-E India: some Conceptual Issues

The Dependency Theory

Dependency theory originated as a challenge from the left to orthodox development theory. In a sense it represents the coming age of social science paradigm by and for the Third World. Its roots are found to in the work of the UN Economic Commission for Latin America (ECLA) in the early 1960s, under the leadership of Argentinean economist Raul Presbisch. He called attention to the deterioration in the terms of trade for producers of primary products and sought redress in Latin America through economic integration. The search for means of understating modern processes of perpetuating exploitative relations between First World and Third World was carried on by other Latin Americans, notably Brazilians Fernando Henrique Cardoso and Teotonio dos Santos and Chilean Osvaldo Sunkel, along German-American Andre Gunder Frank.

The Dependency theorists see development in the center of the world capitalist system (the industrialized countries) and under-development in the periphery (less developed, or backward, countries) as two sides of the same coin. In their view development of the center has occurred and still does at the expense of (and indeed, because of) underdevelopment in the periphery. *Dependentistas* reject Marx's famous assertion that "the country that is more developed industrially only shows, to the less developed, the image of its own future". For dependency theory Less Developed Countries (LDC) see the image of their future in the mirror- it is themselves. They will never become "developed" unless they can break out of the imperialist world system that relegates them to a subordinate.

Dependency theory is so named because its adherents believe that certain countries (those of Third World) are dependent on others, in the sense that they cannot experience any self- sustaining growth, or expansion, but can only grow and change as a reflection of the expansion of those countries that dominate them (the advanced countries). That is why the Third World countries are not undeveloped, but *underdeveloped.*

Dependency theorists have offered several arguments to explain why the development of the advanced capitalist countries produces underdevelopment in the Third World.

Dependency theory starts with the presumption that capitalist economy cannot reproduce itself. It must reach out to other social formations and use them, either as market or as source of extra profit, in order to survive and grow. Some *dependentistas* and their intellectual ancestors stress the role of the Third World as a market for the excess of commodities that is produced in the advanced countries but cannot be sold there. While looking from a historical vantage point at the problem of overproduction (or "underconsumption") in the developed countries, they argue that with the introduction of machinery on a large scale, workers are displaced from the production process. As the rank of unemployment swells, the demand for consumer goods falls (or at least does not grow). Since the aim of the capitalist is to keep wages low and to try to hold down their consumption (in order reinvest later), as output grows the demand for final goods and services cannot keep up. Therefore, the underconsumptionist contend, capitalists must seek external markets for the surplus they cannot sell at home. Many argue that the laws of motion of capitalist development dictate the need for an ever-expanding market; rivalry among imperialist powers develops over control of external markets in the colonies, which are non-capitalist. This rivalry gave rise to World War I and World War II.

However, the dependency literature more commonly portrays the Third World as source of profits that accrue to developed country capitalists, either because of their direct transfers, such as license payments, loyalties, or remittances of profits on direct investment, or because of cheap raw materials or labour from the Third World are used to produce commodities for sale in the developed countries. The idea that a portion of surplus produced by LDCs is extracted and used by the developed countries (DCSs) to fuel their own expansion is present in the works of nearly all the dependency writers.

Major Tenets of Dependency Theory

Surplus Extraction

Almost all the dependency theorists believe that the origin and perpetuation of underdevelopment in the Third World is mainly the result of the extraction of surplus from LDCs. The mechanism by which this extraction is supposed to occur varies from monopoly power to unequal exchange. Most dependenistas agree that the advanced countries of Western Europe and North America developed by looting and plundering the countries of Africa, Asia and Latin America.

Dependency theorists argue that the extraction of surplus continues today in the form of repatriated profits. Thus according to the dependency theorists, growth in the developed countries comes about, not because of exploitation of workers in the developed countries (as Marx argued), but on the basis of exploitation of the underdeveloped countries.

The Monthly Review School

One group of dependency theorists has become known as the *Monthly Review* School, because of their association with that journal and the influence of its editors (Sweezy and Magdoff) on them. The writers of the *Monthly Review* School, which include Frank, Baran, Magdoff, and Amin, generally agree that the LDCs remain backward because a large portion of their surplus product is siphoned off by foreign capital, rather than being reinvested, as they believe it would in the absence of foreign control over industry.

The work of the *Monthly Review* School writers highlights the facts that the LDCs are dependent on foreign capital for technology, management, markets for exports, financing etc. According to these writers, this dependence guarantees that the surplus produced in the LDCs will flow to the DCSs in the form of license payments, profits, interests, and terms of trade that are unfavorable to the LDCs.

Baran, Sweezy, and Magdoff in particular are famous for the emphasis they play on the role of monopoly power in the organization of the capitalist world economy. They point out that the subsidiaries of the multinational corporations (MNCs) from the developed countries maintain internal monopolies in underdeveloped countries. Theses farms do not compete, innovate, or expand production levels. They keep other capitalists out of the underdeveloped countries, fix prices at high levels and pay low wages in order to maximize profits, which are then repatriated to the developed countries. In such a situation dependency theorist find no wonder industrialization in the LDCs.

Unequal Exchange

A variant of the surplus extraction thesis (put forward by Arghiri Emmanuel, Samir Amin, and Ernest Mandel) is based on the idea that the underdeveloped countries are kept underdeveloped by virtue of unequal exchange with the developed capitalist countries. This theory holds that the trading relationships between developed and underdeveloped countries result in a transfer of surplus out of the underdeveloped countries. Rather than focusing on the repatriation of profits actually earned in the periphery, the theory of unequal exchange looks at the transfer of potential profits from the periphery to the center. Through these mechanisms surplus production in the periphery is realized as profit in the center.

Emmanuel's Model

Arghiri Emmanuel seeks to show that unequal exchange forms the basis for uneven development among countries in the world economy. To prove his point he constructs a model of unequal exchange, which at first seems very similar to Ricardo's wine-cloth model of comparative advantage, with one major modification. He argues that while labor is still not mobile internationally, capital is perfectly mobile. He also assumes that producers in both developed and underdeveloped countries have access to the same technology, and that labour is equally productive everywhere.

He treats real wages as fixed, with those in the underdeveloped countries fixed at lower level. As a result of the wage differential, products from the advanced (high wage) countries are said to be more expensive and those from the underdeveloped (low wage) countries cheaper than they would be if the wage level were same everywhere.

According to Emmanuel Arghiri, if such were not the case, profits would tend to be higher in the periphery (because of the lower wage prevailing there, and other assumption already listed). The lure of higher profits would then spark a movement of capital from center to the periphery. The resulting increase in the output in the periphery would cause prices to fall there, while the decline in output in the center would lead to an increase in prices there. This process would continue until the rate of profit equalized across countries. Therefore, he concludes that when exchange takes place between developed and underdeveloped countries, it must be an "unequal" exchange. The wage differential ensures that more labor time is expended in the production of those commodities in which the periphery specializes than is used to produce the goods from the center for which they are exchanged.

He believes that trade unions and political action taken by the workers in the advanced countries help to raise wages there and keep them high. He argues that in addition to generating high levels of income and consumption through unequal exchange, high wages also fuel economic expansion in the developed countries by creating a large market and encouraging investment in labour- saving techniques that raise productivity. In the low-wage countries of periphery, the opposite situation is the rule.

Amin's Model

Amin accepts Emmanuel's theory of unequal exchange, but he adds his own explanation of unequal specialization of production on a world scale. His model is enriched with an analysis of class relations in LDCs, largely borrowed from Baran, and links to Marxian theory of crisis. His arguments are often extremely complex, especially when compared with the simplicity of Emmanuel's model.

Amin argues that international trade is not characterized by complex specialization. He notices that the same commodities are often produced in and traded by both low-wage and high-wage countries. According to him, unequal exchange can occur whenever the difference in wage rates is greater than the difference in labour productivities between countries. Because wages are low in the periphery, profit rates tend to be higher. As capital moves from center seeking greater profits, profits rates are equalized and unequal exchange occurs.

However, Amin feels that since the size of the market is so small in the periphery (as a consequence of low wages), capital inflows are too small to have much effect on accumulation in the periphery. In his view, external economies (such as skilled labour, infrastructure etc.) available to capital in the center also help save off flow of capital to the periphery. In addition, Amin argues that balance of payments constraints limit the ability of capital to move to the periphery and produce for export. Very large exports of productive capital to the periphery and the export of large numbers of productive capital would lead to balance of payment deficits for the center.

Amin argues that capital from the center also moves to the periphery to protect the internal dynamics of capitalist accumulation in the center. Capital from the center will undertake production of "peripheral" commodities or close substitutes for them using techniques that involve greater productivity (lower cost). Production of such commodities may be undertaken either in the periphery or in the core itself. Either way, the existence of more efficient export by the periphery is kept low, maintaining favourable conditions for capitalist accumulations in the center.

As a result of the process that Amin describes, production in the periphery has a dual character – backward and advance production (both for export and for domestic market) exists side by side. Amin argues that in the periphery the wage rate is not related to the level of development of the forces of production. He believes that pre-capitalists relations of production in the periphery are maintained by capital in order to ensure supply of cheap labour. In Amin's view capitalism, if labour power is reproduced under pre-capitalist relations, that is, if workers need for food, shelter, etc. are met outside the market economy (through peasant household production, for example), then the cost of reproduction of labour power will be lower, and therefore, labour will be "cheap".

Dependent Capitalist Development

There are *dependentistas* who readily recognize development in the industrial development of the Third World. However, they argue that the type of industrialization that take place in the Third World countries only serves to reproduce and strengthen the relations of dependence between periphery and core. Peripheral industrialization is not independent or self-sustaining, but rather a "distorted", incomplete, dependent form of development. One of the principal forms of dependent development, stressed by F.H. Cardoso, is that capital goods producing sections in the LDCs is either absent or too weak to ensure continuous expansion of the less developed economy. This makes even the most "developed" of the Third World countries inneed of technology transfer.

Those who support the notion of dependent development point out that in the LDCs growth has been concentrated largely in the import-substitution, luxury goods industries, or labour-intensive manufactures for export. Third World goods industrialization is still based on low wages, foreign technology, and surplus extraction. Another dependent development argument, associated with Furtado, holds that inequality of income and wealth distribution that developed during colonization stimulated demand for luxury goods that require capital-intensive technology. This technology generates few jobs, so the mass of people are unemployed or marginally employed and cannot meet their basic needs. The size of the home market is limited in the LDCs, thus limiting industrialization.

The Center-Periphery Model and World Systems Theory

The relationships hypothesized or described by dependency theorists have been incorporated by Norwegian scholar Johan Galtung into a model of elegant simplicity. According to the Centre-Periphery Model, elites of the center, or metropolis draw bounty of their own state system (through taxes, for example) in order to be able to nurture and support co-opted elites of client or "peripheral" states. In turn elites of those clients states dependent upon the elites of the center for assistance in exploiting and suppressing their own peripheral populations, have no choice but to allow center elites to participate in or share in the product of the exploitation of the peripheral peoples of the peripheral states.

World systems theory, pioneered by Immanuel Wallerstein, also views the world economy as segmented into core and periphery areas. Rather than focusing on interactions among governments, however, this approach calls attention to the transnational interactions of non-state actors, particularly the multinational corporations and banks. The international economy is said to be driven by economic elites, particularly of the developed capitalist states, whose governments normally do their bidding. The control centers of the world economy are then the financial rather than the political capitals. The farther one lives from such a center, the lesser is trickle down effect.

Wallerstein, who sees the ideas of *dependentistas* as generally falling within the world systems perspective, takes issue with more traditional approach. That is, both schools assume that each nation-state must pass through the same set of stages, or modes of extracting surplus, in the same order. As he sees it, the nation-state system, which came into being in part as a convenience to economic elites of an earlier era, has ceased to the institutional base of the global economy. The essential struggle, then, is not between rich and poor states, but rather between rich and poor classes in global society.

Linking NEI to Dependency

The NEI occupying the corner of India is one of the most underdeveloped regions of the country. The region does not fit into popular images of other regions of India. It is a region of high hills and steep valleys separated from the mainland by the chicken's neck (which forms only one percent common boundary with the mainland). People living in the small towns and homesteads are ignored by state government and controlled by the bureaucrats and politicians staying in the urban center of Delhi. Unemployment rates exceed those in the rest of the country (for example the most prosperous state of the region Assam has the second highest unemployment rate in the country) and basic facilities for leading a meaningful life are grossly lacking.

The framework of core-periphery can be applied in interpretation of local and social relations producing a place like the NEI. The NEI is not simply sites where people experience the structure and processes of world economy as mediated by the nation-state. How did this region with its condition come to be and what sorts of social relations contributed to this construction? For answering such questions the concept of core-periphery relations come handy for an understanding of the historical development of NEI within the capitalist world economy.

Placing NEI in the World-System

Core-peripheries relations operate at all scales and are active in the production of material inequalities between zones ranging from supranational to the sub-national in scale. A lack of economic diversity and production processes incorporating low wages and relatively simple technologies tend to be the characteristic zones at the peripheral end of the relationship. Conversely, areas at the core exhibit social relations of production typified by higher wages, advanced technology and the production of diverse range of goods (Taylor, 1989). Furthermore, capital-labour relations in peripheries are likely to be more coercive than those found in cores (Wallerstein1974). Wallerstein's third or middle zone; the semi periphery, is made up of places that are on both ends of core-periphery relations. In other words, some places serve both as cores to peripheries and peripheries to the cores.

The core-periphery relations create, maintain and are produced by these unequal material conditions between cores and peripheries. This does not mean that the geography of cores and peripheries is fixed. The particular social and spatial configurations created by core-periphery and class relations change over time without changing these underlying structures of the world–economy (Soja, 1989).

In NEI region, the core-based ownership and control of significant portion of the mineral resources, land and industrial base serves to exact surplus value and remove the functions, processes and the power of ownership. It is this type of relationship, which has helped to create and maintain the relatively limited, low-wage production processes found in the region. The historical development of these socio-spatial relations might lead to the suggestions that place like NEI are in the world economy's periphery.

It will be an exaggeration to say that a region like NEI is part of a peripheral region in the world-economy. But such a designation ignores the complexities introduced by NEI's development as a place within the larger political and economic entity, the Indian State. This development begins with the region's initial absorption into the world –economy as a marginal periphery, a part of the frontier of the British Raj. It eventually leads to the region's peripheral position within a nation-state that, as a whole, is defined as a core by its relation to the world economy. In other words, NEI as a region in the capitalist world-system can only be understood in the context of India's path from periphery to hegemony. Therefore, it will be better to understand how state actions and policies can alter the material conditions, which result from core-periphery and class relations.

From its origin in Europe during the 15th century, the capitalist world-system has grown spatially to encompass the entire globe. The social processes by which regions and their inhabitants are drawn into world-system are known, generally as incorporation. Incorporation is the integration of a region's production process into the interdependent network of production that constitutes the world market (Wallerstein and Martin, 1979). This transforms the region from part of the external arena into a peripheral region of the world-economy. However, the nature of incorporation varies greatly over time and space as the above definition excludes where the contact with the world-system has occurred but where capitalist relations of production have not replaced those existing prior to contact.

Hall (1986) conceptualizes this by formulating a continuum of relations between core areas and the areas being drawn into the world-economy. At one end of this continuum is the eternal arena, which has no relations with any part of the world-system. A contact with periphery is tied into the world-economy only weakly and the core-periphery relations that exist are such that while major social and economic changes occur in the contact periphery, effects in the core are negligible. Full incorporation begins in marginal peripheries as capitalist relations of production replace indigenous modes and the peripheral region becomes more important to the core. Peripherilization is achieved when a region's production processes are completely connected to the world-system and exchange between core and fully dependent periphery becomes important to continued development in the world.

The area of NEI that underwent into the possession of the colonizers, the production process were not altered but completely displaced and removed to the interior. Thus it is a probable that that as a part of the world-economy during the colonial period was incorporated as a marginal periphery. Full peripherialization did not take place until when India began to move from the semi periphery to the core. The actions of the Indian State that both aid and limit NEI's development are among the most important reasons why its position within the world-economy cannot simply be termed peripheral. It becomes that necessity to clarify how socio-spatial relations within a nation-state operate.

Core-periphery relations and the zones that both create and are created by them are nested at different scales. An internal periphery like the NEI is underdeveloped by the socio-economic relations between the residents of the region and core of the world-system. However, the material conditions resulting from these core-periphery relations are altered by core positions of the Indian State as a whole. When the State moves from core to hegemony it tries to extend the space of the periphery. For example the big cities like Guwahati and Shillong in NEI acts as semi periphery to the core but it acts as a core to the region. There are peripheral small towns in the region, which serve these big cities. However, this core-periphery chain doesn't stop here. There has been a further enhancement of the space to places, which may be called as sub peripheries.

On the World Economy's Frontier

Hills, sub-montanneous areas and valley regions of NEI were drawn into the world –economy by the Britishers through the introduction of tea plantation. After the Anglo-Burma War, the Lakhimpur district of Assam was considered an ideal location for colonization by the colonial rulers, as tea bushes were discovered in this sparsely located territory, as a potential cash crop for investment. This resulted in an organized expansion of the tea plantation economy on a technically primitive base. The vast wasteland lying throughout the stretches of Brahmaputra Valley were acquired through different land reform policies always in favor of the colonizers. The easy access to land gave rise to speculative element, which adversely effected the overall production of the region. Land which was acquired at exceptionally low rates was cleared without much concern for demand of regional ecology, resulting in the rapid deterioration of the potentialities of the future plant growth on the one hand, and on the other prevented the use by villagers of their timber and other fuel products. All this led to a period referred to in the contemporary accounts, of 'Tea Mania'. It also led indirectly to indigenous aspirants being left out of this commercial venture. The surplus exploited was partly transferred to the home country, partly invested in military and bureaucratic machinery to sustain and extend territorial aggrandizement, and partly to strengthen the sources of revenue through public investment in railways etc.

A far- reaching process was introduced in terms of capital and house taxes. Most of the hill region except the upper ridges of Arunachal Pradesh was brought within the British fold through the introduction of cash economy in the traditional trade and unequal exchange. The colonial powers introduced the manufactured, glamorized, finished products, which easily attracted the hill people and created a demand for such goods at the big fairs. The tribes became frequent visitor to the fairs and became more dependent on imported goods. The merchant class introduced by the colonizers introduced opium selling and in turn acquired natural products produced by the hill people such as rubber, timber etc. The dependence of the tribes in finished imported goods and opium led to the destructive mode of acquiring resources and eventually led to the depletion of traditional resource base.

Britishers also brought the political, cultural and economic ideals of its own society, which was evident by the establishments of market centers, residential schools, mills, stores and other familiar institutions of modern capitalist society. Administrative headquarters like Shillong and Guwahati and trade centers for newly found oil and tea like Dibrugarh, Jorhat and Tezpur and health centers were established. The spread of Christian Missionary activity especially in hill areas of Mizoram, Meghalaya and Nagaland made primary education fairly widespread in these areas. Markets towns and colonies were the physical artifacts of social relations transplanted in to the region. These served to connect the frontier to the expanding world-system.

For the first few decades of the colonial rule, India remained as a part of the world-system's periphery by its relation with the core powers in Europe, particularly Great Britain. Within India the NEI region remained on the margins of the world-economy. In the later half of colonial period India began to develop its own manufacturing industries. However, this kind of industrialization did not have any effect on north-eastern part of the country. This was the early example of local initiative forced by the developed pockets of India as a marginal periphery in the world-economy to reproduce a relationship of dependency with the residents of city closer to the world -system's core.

From Frontier to Internal Periphery

The opening up of the local barrier to trade by the Britishers led to a flow of migration to the region. In fact it was part of the colonial policy to introduce an intermediary class as the colonial policy discouraged the local entrepreneurs. With the development of rail lines and roads and flourishing of extractive enterprises like tea, oil and plywood the streams of migration continued in the region. Often working through local elites, these absentee interests had the financial resources that local capitalist lacked, and therefore, were able to acquire thousands of acres of timber lands and mineral rights and set up saw meals, coal business and other enterprises. Thus core-based interests acquired the lion's share of land resources, built the facilities needed to extract timber and coal and sold their products and households in the core. It was this form of core-periphery relations varying in time and space with local circumstances that created the NEI an internal periphery during the last half of 19th century and opening decades of 20th century. However, these enterprises were not fully independent as these formed part of the market center at the national level. While some small operations were locally owned, the majority of the resources and the largest numbers of workers were controlled by non-residents. However, through all these the local residents were not passively experiencing peripherialization. They were actors in these relations forming the region. While most were workers who had left farms or migrated into the areas, a few were long time owners of large property who profit by selling lands and mineral rights to the core-based investors hoping to exploit the timber-covered and coal-filled mountains. Certainly, some residents acquired a fair amount of wealth and power by being the local representatives or agents of the absentee-owned timber, coal, tea and other resources. In their efforts to develop the region, these local elites continued to reproduce the core-periphery relations that were developing in the place. However, the formation of elite and middle class owes much of administrative jobs and rather than their involvement in the resource sector.

Restructuring and Federal Interventions

Using various institutions and policies national government attempted both to improve the country's position in the world-economy and to mitigate or amplify the impacts of the global capitalist system have on various places within their jurisdictions. Planning was initiated as instrument for attaining balanced growth and in order to ensure that the country within the world-economy maintains minimum standard of living in the relatively poor places. In the 70s the government began to recognize that the inhabitants of certain places and regions were not included in the new affluent society. Towards this the NEI has been identified as a 'problem region' that was left behind.

The North Eastern region was reorganized in 1971 and full-fledged states like Meghalaya, Tripura and Manipur were created along with Union Territories of Arunachal Pradesh and Mizoram. The North Eastern Council (N.E.C.) came into being in the wake of re-organization and was conceived as catalytic agent to bring about integrated development of backward units. The Council owing a Presidential order was formally inaugurated on 7th November, 1972 by the then Prime Minister of India Mrs. Indira Gandhi. Inaugurating the Council she said, "The primary purpose of the Council is the development of the region for greater human welfare…I should like the Council to draw up projects which will benefit more one unit…I am glad to inaugurate this Council which is a promising innovation in regional planning. May it will fulfill the hope we have invested in it."

The main thrust of the Council's policies and programmes was rapid and balanced development of the region through programmes of regional importance concerning all or more than one state territory, it was to supplement the efforts of their respective areas by rendering them such balancing and infrastructural support as they needed.

However, after few years of its emergence there was cynicism among people about the role it was playing. A noted journalist associated with the region M. S. Prabhakar mentions in one of his writings regarding the formation of N.E.C. that "on the face of it is difficult to see the rational behind the formation of the North Eastern Council which came into existence on 1st August, 1972 and was formally inaugurated by the Prime Minister on November 7th, 1972. After the reorganization of the North Eastern region, it was considered necessary to have coordinating body for this region; Zonal Council in terms of Article 15-22 of States Reorganization Act of 1956 could have been formed.... North Eastern Council seeks out merely usurp the limited powers of the states, but to totally replace the authority of the states by the Centre, especially by the most repressive organs of the states of the region by their reduction to total impotence." Prabhakar commented that it is very difficult to see the rational behind the formation of the NEC. The whole idea of integrated development and coordinated development of specific areas is faulty and the Council is merely a decorative body.

The N.E.C. adopted a highly bureaucratic and technological approach in its pursuit for finding regional policies for the region. It spends major portion of its plan outlay in developing infrastructure and assumes that by taking care of infrastructural development it can achieve regional development. However, authors like Munshi, Guha and Chaube (1978) have shown that infrastructural indices associated with modernization have no correlation with the actual growth indices in the units of NEI. With its overemphasis on infrastructure accompanied with a half-hearted concern the N.E.C failed to create human capacity formation for a balanced regional development.

The failure in developing the local forces of production led the region increasingly dependent on the mainland. In the absence of industrialization despite the abundance of prime resources like oil, timber, tea, gas, limestone, water and forest wealth the region became an ideal market for manufactured goods from industrial parts of India and new industries and jobs were created outside the region. The major portion of savings of people of the region is spent on buying smallest consumable items. The Shukla Commission estimated that about Rs. 2,500 crore worth of consumables is imported form outside the region every year. For example Assam imports 74 percent of its milk products, 94 percent of its eggs and 98 percent of its meat requirements from outside. The region is blessed with water resources, yet it imports half its fish requirements from outside. In addition, the credit –deposit ratio being very low in the region, the banking sector transfers something like Rs 5,000 crore from this region to other regions for investment.

The trade and industries have been controlled by a floating migrant population, which enjoys exclusive monopoly. Major industries of the region like tea, oil, plywood is the in the hand of the big Indian bourgeoisie. For example out of about 620 tea gardens in the Brahmaputra Valley, only Assamese planters own about 158. The Monopoly Inquiry Commission of 1965 declared that there are 24 factories in Assam belonging to the top 75 business groups in the private sector and almost all these factories are located in the tea gardens (Misra, 1980). The total annual profit from the tea in the 80s was several times more than the total annual revenue receipts of the state. The state of Assam is entitled to an agricultural tax imposed on 60 percent of the profit from tea gardens, while the Central government is entitled to an income tax 40 percent of the total profit. However because of the widespread practice of the Indian and the foreign capital to conceal major share of their profit, this has been robbing the state as well as the Central government of their share of revenue and taxes.

Moreover, though the 756 tea gardens in Assam account for about 55 percent of the tea produced in India and earn an annual Rs.500 crore as foreign exchange for the country, except for the newly-formed Assam Tea Corporation which is a public sector organization owning a few sick and unprofitable tea gardens, the overwhelming majority of the big gardens are under the foreign and Indian companies which are controlled from London and Calcutta. The main office of the Tea Board, which is the highest authority in relation to the tea industry and which, besides implementing the Tea Act of 1958, is also responsible for approving grants, loans and labour welfare projects, is situated in Calcutta though most of the gardens are in Assam. Assam did not have a tea auction center till the mid 80s. Since the major portion of tea was sold in the Calcutta the state all these years was loosing the vital sale tax on tea. The manufacturing plants paid low wages to the workers and had few, if any linkages to the local farms. Thus core-based companies, which owned these plants, simply used the labor of an internal periphery to reduce their operating cost.

Assam has an estimated reserve of 70.46 million tones of crude oil and 23,000 cubic metres of natural gas. The oilfields of upper Assam produce about 43 lakh tones of crude oil and since this crude has a very high aromatic content, it is rated high in the world market. According to the international price standards, Assam crude should cost 1.5 times more higher than the low grade OPEC (ibid). However, there was no refinery till the 80s and crude was carried through pipeline to the refinery in Barauni in Bihar. The Central Government refuses to fix the royalty rates on Assam crude at 20 percent of the posted price of equivalent of Middle East crude in India. Even in sales tax that Assam derives from her crude is Rs.54 per tones whereas India gets Rs. 991 per tone as sale tax on Assam crude (ibid).

The 70s and 80s witnessed the consolidation of middle and elite class in the region. With the penetration of capital in the tribal areas a new tribal elite class came up. Acting to further their own interests, many of these elite and middle classes started organizing the local based support. But question arises where do these elite and middle class act. Definitely it is in the sub peripheries where they mobilize their bases. Sub peripheries are the peripheries of sub centers. Due to low urbanization and low level of industrialization the capitalist economy having a number of dependent and domestic modes of production unevenly distributed over the space in NEI looks beyond the peripheries to open up to the logic of metropolis Pan-Indian market. The big cities like Guwahati and Shillong act as the semi peripheries to the Indian core but to NEI region these cities act as core to the middle level townships (mostly the district head quarters and trade centers). Beyond these are the small townships, which are more in numbers and form the peripheries. But there is marginal space i.e. the sub peripheries beyond the peripheries and these markets have become the target for the expanding economy in the absence of urbanization.

The sub peripheries are characterized by the overwhelming presence of the intermediary class. It is the space where the products of domestic modes of production are exchanged. This presence of a parasitic class like the petty traders, and moneylenders tilts the exchange process to an unequal exchange. For example most of the forest resources located in the sub peripheral areas in NEI region have passed from the hands of local people to the hands of unscrupulous traders who are engaged in large- scale timber extraction for meeting the needs of the urban areas and industries. In the case of Arunachal, Mishra (1983) notes that being a very highly forest dependent economy, the traditional communal form of forest use has changed a great deal with the opening of market networks for forest producers, particularly for timber. The emergence of group of prosperous, upwardly mobile, forest contractors acting as intermediaries between outside businessmen and local communities, is the most important outcome of timber trade. This has changed the occupational structure of the tribals and a rural labor market has come up in the remotest places of Arunachal. The process of forest wood use has also undergone remarkable change. The sub peripheries of Arunachal, which provide tribal to the access of forest products such as firewood; bamboo etc. have undergone deforestation and depletion of the forest and have immensely affected the earnings and survival strategies of the tribal poor. So, under such a system of forest utilization, the forest dwellers are reduced to the status of casual wage laborers who became increasingly dependent on the consumption items made available by the core-based industries in the local market through the linkage of periphery and semi periphery.

The sub peripheral areas are also witnessing the flourishing of the informal credit market in the presence of the moneylenders. In micro study carried out from five villages of Lakhimpur district of upper Assam, Kuri (2001) found that the practice of usufructuary mortgage has led to land alienation of the rural masses in the absence of developed and transparent credit market. According to the findings of the study more than 96 percent of the of the credit contracts under the system of land mortgage is under the non-complete form of usufructuary mortgage. Under the system the lenders enjoy the usufructs of the mortgaged land till the repayment of loan. The interest charged for lending money is extremely high. Small farmers usually borrow a large amount of money through land mortgage, mainly for consumption, housing, medical and ceremonial uses. Since most of the credit is used for non-productive purposes a greater risk of defaulting exists and a defaulting of loan leads to land alienation. This kind of credit transaction has brought an increasing land alienation and greater dependence of small and marginal farmers to the moneylenders.

This kind of depressing situation has been further aggravated by strategy, programmes and policy frame adopted for the development of the region in general and sub peripheries in particular. The programmes place too much reliance on the selected groups of people who are expected to actively participate in development efforts. They also place too much on the growth linkages with core and semi peripheral markets, commercialization of skills and designs, mechanization of agriculture and the basic changes in the concept of property ownership. In this type of situation the capitalist economy extracts the maximum benefit, and the domestic economy increases its dependence on these agents. The forces generated by the nature of new economic planning have completely subordinated the interests of the marginal groups and restricted local control over resources. Thus, the crucial element in such developmental measures has been a shift from 'primitive independence' to 'complete dependence'.

The growing internal differentiation in the sub peripheries has given a fillip to the already existing underlying class structure. The accumulation of profit in the hands of few in the sub peripheries gave an upper hand in mobilization of the marginal groups. The arguments for establishing new state or country received local support because people imagined themselves as forming a new place, a new community. These sub peripheries were turned into spaces of mobilizing marginal groups on cultural and geographical markers. With intensification of such movements insurgency began to grow in these areas under those circumstances. It is in the sub peripheries that most of the insurgency movements have their base.

Boosterism and Restructuring: the Post Reform Period

Post reform period the Indian economy witnessed the recession and continuous restructuring. The new Economic Policy came with the opening up of the economy and new intervention in the form of 'package programme' began for the region. The announcement of the new packages mostly coincided with the change of power in New Delhi. By 90s the region witnessed already several military operation against various insurgent groups. In fact the 90s witnessed a proliferation of insurgency groups with the intensification of subperipherilization of the region's economy.

The new economy took the shape of a 'terrorist economy' or an 'underground economy' with the increasing alignment of terrorist groups with the bureaucracy due to the breakdown of civil governance and a systematic corruption started in the region of looting the public exchequer. A complex collusive arrangement between various legitimate power elites and terrorist groupings exists in every single theatre of terrorist strife in the Northeast and this arrangement facilitates a continuous transfer of resources into the underground economy. The situation, in fact, realizes the worst-case scenario, where "the political establishment and the mafia reach a collusive agreement in order to share the rents from the monopolistic provision of public services" (Sahni, 2000). The result is that the vast official machinery uses its authority to appropriate a large segment of the States' revenues, and distributes it within a nexus of politicians, administrators and banned militant organizations, often with the mediation of a variety of contractors and commercial front organizations of the terrorists themselves. The subversion of the Public Distribution System (PDS) in Assam provides an interesting example. The bulk of the commodities available in the PDS scheme have been diverted to the open market generating large illegal revenues, large proportion of which goes to the banned terrorist outfit. 'Rural development' is another lucrative sector, and it is estimated that as much as 70 per cent of all funds available to the State government in Assam under this head is systematically siphoned off under a well organized network of militant outfits, contractors, civil servants (ibid). All government contracts in terrorism affected sub peripheral areas in the Northeast have been completely monopolized by contractors who front for, or work under the 'protection' of extremist groups.

In the wake of globalization and because of the softening of geo-political rigidities following India's recent understanding with China a new approach has been forwarded as a panacea for the underdevelopment i.e. the *Look East* Approach. In this approach lately there has been a talk of converting the locational disadvantage of the region into a boon by integrating the regional economy with the world economy. All the seven states of NEI region form international borders opening up trade and commerce with South Asia and South East Asia has been proposed by the policy makers. Most of the policy makers in the region are excited and optimistic about the idea of linking their economies with the dynamic Asia. There have been suggestions like if the Indian Government is reluctant to open up the natural trade routes, the states in NEI region should ask the Central government to compensate for their loss of trade. In recent years there has been much emphasis on the part of the Indian government on investing on infrastructure to develop NEI region. There have been even ambitious efforts to its natural markets in south-east Asia by building roads through Myanmar. Recently the border road (the Tamu-Kalewa) has been made open for trade.

There has widespread difference of opinion among development experts regarding the opening up the border and its linkage with the development of the region. There exists widespread difference between the agenda of state and the common people from the region. The Indian State seems to look at the issue of border opening from the point of view of trade and its concomitant linkage with the national economy. Whereas scholars from NEI region question whether opening up of international border can solve critical issues like refugee infiltration, labour migration, the protection of local producers and environmental degradation. Scholars like Sanjib Baruah (2002) believes that improving infrastructure will not automatically guarantee that the people of NEI region will be benefited from it. He believes that the decision to investment on infrastructure should be based on their "social rates of return". The moot question here is that whether the control over land, resources, ideas and people would remain in the hands of the Indian state which privileges the pan-Indian point of view at the expense of the regional one. Here Baruah (2002) feels that a weak Indian State disembedded from the NEI society is hardly in a position to take care of the interests of issues of small marginal producers of the region. Meanwhile another native scholar Hazarika (2001) looks at the issue from the point of view of infiltration and labour migrations considered as one of the most critical issues for any permanent development solution for the state of Assam. According to him the border between Assam and the neighboring country Bangladesh is an administration's imagination. There has been continuous flow of illegal migrants from Bangladesh, a country ravaged by natural calamity, acute poverty and high population pressure in different periods of time. Because of this illegal proxy trade cropped up and the both the central government and the NEI are region loosing vital revenue. Hazarika (2001) suggests that opening up of the border and regularization of labour migration through providing job permits and identity cards and better policing in the border can be a solution to the illegal migration.

So, the policies to help to reformat the region's economy reproduce the core-periphery relations influencing activities in every major sector of the region's economic base. While core-periphery relations extract surplus from the region, which gets accumulated to other cores of the nation, the region continues to lie in the periphery of the nation in terms of social and economic status. Of course, many of the development programmes and other welfare efforts would not have been possible without the aid from the Central government. However, the development

Table No. 2
Net Domestic Product and Per Capita Income (at current prices) of North-Eastern States.

State	1980-81		1985-86		1996-97	
	State income (Rs. In millions)	Per Capita Income (Rs.)	State income (Rs. In millions)		State income (Rs. In milions)	Per Capita Income (Rs.)
1	2	3	4	1	2	3
Arunachal Pradesh	873	1,382	2,024	Arunachal Pradesh	873	1,382
Assam	23,978	1,221	44,773	Assam	23,978	1,221
Manipur	1,973	1,382	3,816	Manipur	1,973	1,382
Meghalaya	1,494	1,131	3,153	Meghalaya	1,494	1,131
Mizoram	620	1,289	1,570	Mizoram	620	1,289
Nagaland	1,024	1,1351	2,420	Nagaland	1,024	1,1351
Tripura	2,451	1,211	4,850	Tripura	2,451	1,211
All India	11685	1,627	206133	All India	11685	1,627

Soruces: 1. *Basic Statistics,* NE Region, North Eastern Coouncil, 1995,p.169
2. Economic of Survey India, 1999-2000, pp. S-11-12

intervention of the Center and State fails to have impact on the region as these welfare interventions overlooks the dependent structure underlying in the economy and unfortunately reproduces the same dependent structure.

Some Indicators of Underdevelopment in NEI

One of the most striking facts about the various indicators of welfare in the NEI region is trailing behind in almost all the indicators from the rest of the country. Notwithstanding, relatively rapid economic growth in India and more so in the post reform period, the pace of growth in the NEI part of India has been almost stagnant and even slowing down with respect to certain sectors of the regional economy. In this sections below vital indicators of the backwardness of the region is discussed.

Slow Growth of State Domestic Product

One of the prominent features of the NEI economy is the slow growth in the State Domestic Product (SDP) and over the years the gap is gradually increasing. Per Capita Income generation and over the years the gap between the region and the national average is increasing. For example in 1950-51, the per capita income in Assam was 4 percent above the national average. In 1998-99 it was 41 percent below the national average at current prices and 45 percent below the national average at 1980-81 prices. Between 1980 and 1990, per capita income at 1980 prices grew by 20 percent in Assam compared with 40 percent for all India. Between 1980 and 1998, per capita income in Assam grew by 10 percent compared with 39 percent for all India (Assam Development Report, 2002).

A cursory look at the data of NSDP of the seven states reveals the fact that the annual average growth rate of NSDP has been gradually declining over the years. Gradual decline of Net State Domestic Product in the 1990's show the nature of dependent accumulation in North-East Region. It shows that the rate of accumulation in North-East has slowed down and reached far below the national average in case of most of the states of North-East. This shows that the State with its leadership in transforming economy in capitalistic modes of production has not fully been able to gear itself up as a manager of 'surplus'. This further means (I) State is not able to enlarge economic surplus (in rural, urban or overall) (II) transfer it among sectors (III) to be extracted so as to compel increases in either size or the proportion of it i.e. inter-sectoral transfers. The decline in NSDP cripples the State from becoming repository of development and potential of productive forces.

Low Per Capita Income

Per capita income, which has been accepted as yardstick of standard of living of the people, in comparison to the national income of North-East there is a large gap between the region's income and the national income. For example in 1950-51, the per capita income in Assam, considered as one of the most prosperous state in the region, was 4 percent above the national average. In 1998-99 it was 41 percent below the national average at current prices and 45 percent below the national average at 1980-81 prices. Between 1980 and 1990, per capita income at 1980 prices grew by 20 percent in Assam compared with 40 percent for all India. Between 1980 and 1998, per capita income in Assam grew by 10 percent compared with 39 percent for all India (Assam Development Report, 2002).

The situation is the same in the other States of the Northeastern region as well. Against the all-India PCI of Rs. 14,712 in 1998-99, as given in the Economic Survey for 2000-2001, Assam's figure was Rs. 8,700, Tripura's was Rs. 9,187, Manipur's was Rs. 10,599, Arunachal's was Rs. 12,929 and Meghalaya's was Rs. 10,607. Mizoram's figure for 1997-98 was Rs. 11,667. No official figures for Nagaland were available. These figures indicate that all States of the Northeastern region are placed below the national average in per capita income. From these data one can infer that for the various classes of the population this decline also shows underdevelopment of productive forces within the mode of production. This further points out that the productive forces are on an external support system.

High Dependence on Agriculture

The economy of the NEI heavily depends upon the agriculture sector. More than 70 percent of the population of the region depends upon on agriculture for its livelihood. Cultivators and agriculture labourers account for 73.8% in Arunachal Pradesh, 65.8% in Assam, 68.7% in Manipur, 73.3% in Nagaland as against 68.5% in all India average as per 1981 Census. The proportion of NEI states is relatively higher than other states like Tamil Nadu, Kerala, Punjab, Gujarat, Haryana and Bengal. The share of percent of agricultural income in the SDP was 48.6% in Assam, 49.3% in Meghalaya, 31.6% in Nagaland, 53.4% in

Manipur and 52.8% in Tripura as against 16.2% in Maharashtra and 27.8% in Tamil Nadu.

High dependence on agriculture in North-East India demonstrates that domestic and peripheral modes of production continues to engage in the larger number of workforces in rural, semi-urban and intermediary transactions of food supply economies. Such economies based on sharecropping and community-holding lands points to an increased pressure on land. The produce of such a mode of production is more or less restricted to producing food for cash cropping peasants and pauperized rural labourers. Local food and surpluses are exported and hence it does not generate money income. Given the incidence of poverty in some of the states of NEI there is periodic shortfall in food supply resulting in shortfall in calorie intake. Absence of industrialization in an appropriate form has further magnified the dependence on the domestic modes of production for the larger section of the populace. The scenario of the peasants in the distress political economy of subsistence is compounded by an absence of industry.

High Dependence on Centre and Low Revenue Generation

The North- Eastern states enjoy some special privileges in the matter of grants and loans from the centre. The low revenue generated from its own sources in its total revenue receipts coupled with the special status enjoyed by the states has led to the over dependence of the states on the centre. For example in the case of Assam the total revenue generated by the State Government is declining from about 40 percent at the beginning of the 90's decade to just 30 percent at the end of it. This is the result of a lower annual growth rate of 12.5% in state's own revenue receipts than that of Central revenue transfers 16.4% (Assam Development Report, 2002). In addition, the composition of central transfers shows a decline in the share of state plan transfers and shared taxes; to be covered up mainly by centrally sponsored schemes and non-plan grants.

The fact of low revenue generation shows that the formal structure of the State cannot appear in increasing portion of the resources collected, by whatever agencies, at the source from the tax payer. The involution of the State and the sphere of public finance can not ensure that for every unit increase in the informal structures, i.e. business houses, farm and producers etc. on whom State has little control, the formal State structure does not have a commensurate increase. It produces the gap between revenues collected by the State and other non-State and informal and socio-economic units. In other words State in the context of NEI cannot develop a formal apparatus of financial responsibility for various section of income generating populace and therefore remains dependent on the center.

High Incidence of Poverty

The states in NEI are characterized by high incidence of poverty, especially rural poverty. The Planning Commission Expert Group headed by Prof. Lakdawala made an estimation of poverty in the region. As per the group 36.5% of the total population of the region is below poverty line (BPL) and the population was only0.38% higher than the national average.

Incidence of poverty is high in the rural areas of North- East. Recent report published by Planning Commission on Assam's Development has shown that while urban poverty has declined smoothly over the period of time but rural poverty has some ups and downs. For example 1987-88 and 1993-94 rural poverty in Assam increased by 5 percentage points while urban poverty declined by 2 percentage points. Within the state however there is a high incidence of poverty in the hill areas. For example National Sample Survey data for two periods 1987-88 and 1993-94 shows that rural poverty in the hill regions doubled in the study period. Rural poverty is highest among the agricultural and other labourers (as high as 76% and 80%) followed by self-employed in agriculture and self –employed in non-agriculture in that order.

High incidence of poverty shows that the proportion which benefits from process of development is very less because the occupational structure remains dependant upon investment from outside. The low yield of productive resources from occupations segmented social structure and favours only a few and those few have a nexus with the market. One can term the situation as a negative growth of market and employment that is the result of the dependent modes of production.

Poor Status of Basic Services

The NEI region is also characterized by the deteriorating living conditions. Health and education related services are low if one compares with the developed states of India like Kerala. Availability of basic services has affected the quality of life in the region. A cursory look at the table No.4 reveals the fact. Here one good example is Assam,

Table No.3.
Gap of Per Capita Income between Assam and India (at constant 1980-81 prices)

Year	1950-51	1960-61	1970-71	1980-81	1990-91	1995-96	1996-97	1997-98
India	1127	1350	1520	1630	2222	2608	2761	3132
Assam	1173	1140	1221	1284	1524	1606	1628	1708
Difference	46(+)	210(-)	299(-)	346(-)	698(-)	1002(-)	1133(-)	1424(-)
Assam/India	1.04	0.84	0.84	0.79	0.62	0.62	0.59	0.55

Source: Planning Commission of India (2002), *Assam Development Report.*

which ranks 12 among 16 states when ordered in descending order of Human Development Index (HDI) and Gender Development Index (GDI). Rural and urban disparity is very high on several of the indicators. Life expectancy at birth is 54.1 in rural as compared 63.3 in urban areas.52% of the children are underweight in rural compared to 37% in urban areas.

The low standard of living symbolizes asymmetries of distribution of the primary goods, which inflicts the apparently modernizing State structure and plural society as well. Low level of standard of living further signifies the structural bottlenecks of growth and mobility. (Table No.4)

These indicators of slow growth of economy are not merely a sectoral manifestations of the process of unequal exchange relations, but the congenital outcome of the staggering antinomies between investment and extraction of surplus. The question is how does extra dose of investment offset the cost of surplus extraction? As surplus extraction is the leading phenomenon, fall in the cost of factors of production can never catch up the volume of direct investment by the State. Rather it is the other way round, with a free bit of investment of Capital there is an increased fall in the cost of raw materials and other factors of production. The poor living conditions of the populace is a mark of reduced income generation which by itself is an indicator of an *in-capability* to hold onto resources that are specific to the region. Poor health and sanitation, malnutrition and absence of essential amenities paradoxically acts as a shield to hide the high rates of surplus extraction and only reveals the necessity of investment for development. This revealed face of necessity of development itself acts as a cloak for the internal process of surplus extraction. It is here that indicators of development remain dangling at the steady process of externalization of basic resources of the economy of NEI.

In terms of modes of production, the poor living condition is a mark of underdevelopment of domestic modes of production. But the historically developed relations of exchange in intermediary and capitalist modes of production demonstrate the in-capability of merging the domestic into it. Rather these modes of production themselves play a subsidiary role in the final outcome of the supply changing from periphery to the core.

Table No. 4
Living Conditions by North-eastern States, 1998-99

State	Percentage Share of Households					
	With Electricity	With Drinking Water that is piped or from a hand pump	With a toilet or latrine	Using biomass fuel for cooking	Living in a pucca house	Mean number of persons per room
India	**60.1**	**77.9**	**35.9**	**71.7**	**32**	**2.7**
Arunachal Pradesh	68.9	80.7	73	80.8	14.2	2.2
Assam	26.4	60.1	63	87.1	10.9	2.1
Manipur	75.3	48.9	92	69.2	7.1	2.1
Meghalaya	41.2	42.1	52	83.5	14.5	2
Mizoram	84.1	63.2	97.7	57.4	16.2	2.6
Nagaland	56.3	40.5	74.3	86.1	18.1	1.6
Sikkim	80.7	84.6	72.7	63.2	50.6	2
Kerala	**71.8**	**19.9***	**85.2**	**81.7**	**79.8**	**1.3**

Source:: Planning Commission of India (2002), *Assam Development Report*

*this figure is low because in Kerala majority of the household obtains their drinking water from wells.

3

Putting 'Space' into Political Economy

North-East India as a Critical Geo-political Region

The Idea of Region

The idea of region can be traced back to the founder of human geography Vidal de Lablache's magnum opus *Tableau del la Geographie de la France*. In his work, Vidal attempted a harmonious blending of physical and human features in the Tableau (France Plateau), which he termed as 'pays' (region). His notion of *pays* is that each pays has its own distinctive agriculture due to its soil and water supply and also due to economic specialization made possible by the demands of people living in town. So in geographical parlance a region came to be identified as an entity consisting of contagious or non-contagious spatial units that are similar to each other in terms of one or more chosen criteria. However, after the Second World War and especially after the Industrial Revolution the concept of region as a spatial unit characterized by unique physical, economic and cultural characteristics began to face criticism due to the development of communication and the concomitant decline of the traditional local self sufficient economy.

In recent time many interesting aspects of the discursive and geographical conjunctions of politics have been put forward in the context of critical geopolitics. Recent writings on critical geopolitics have increasingly highlighted the discourse on the production of political space and to the increasing governmentality of modern society. The new discourse is an attempt to incorporate discourse analytic approach of critical geopolitics with a theoretical framework of looking regions and territories as social constructs. According to it social world is actively constructed is not just passively reflected in knowledge. Furthermore, social space is saturated with meanings that cannot be reduced to our

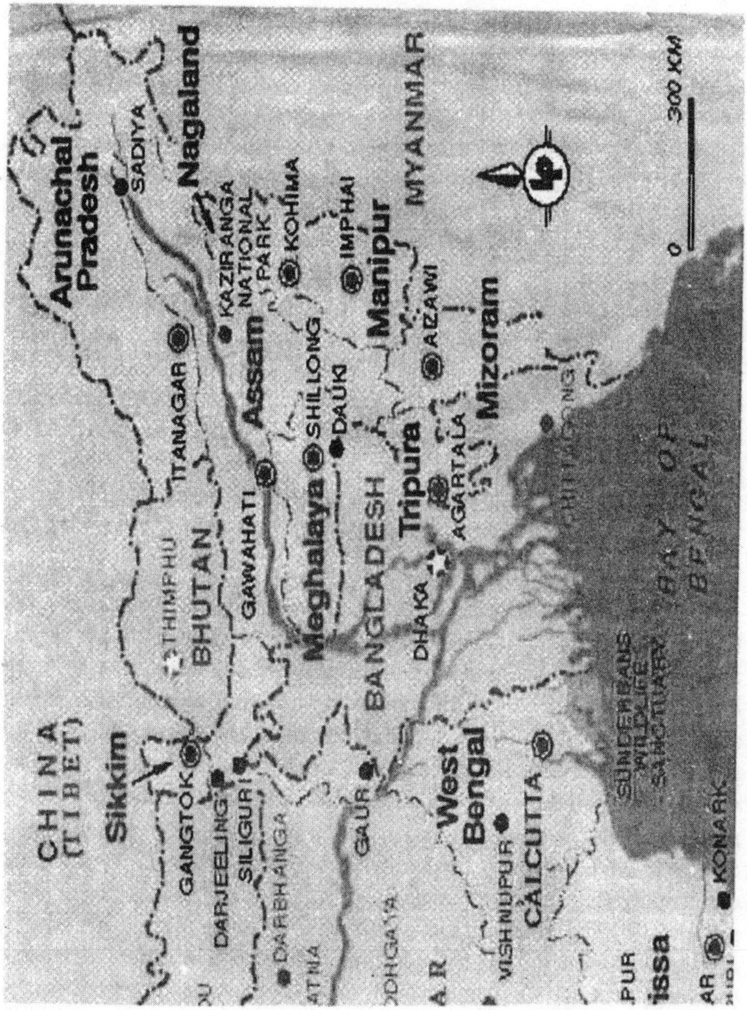

Map 1: The North-East India and its Neighbours

Source: http://www.necouncil.nic.in/

knowledge of it no matter how accurate or 'objective' one thinks that knowledge is. Hence, representatives of space are neither politically innocent nor exhaustive. This idea is crystallized in the notion of "deep space" put forward by Smith (1990) and Gregory (1994). According to them "deep space" is a socially produced space that is constantly negotiated and represented in social practices, but can never be reduced to any single representation of it. The notion of "deep space" recognizes that there are discursive forms of social life which may full outside the ocularcentric grasp of institutional discourses as it does not mean automatic to form any essentialism. "Deep space" according to Smith (1990:160-161) refers not to the sheer immensity of absolute space...explored, defixed, and refined by physics and astronomy, space science and cosmology. Rather it refers to the relativity of the terrestrial space, the space of everyday life, from the global to the local and architectural in which to use Doreen Massey's metaphor 'different layers of life and social landscape are sedimented into each other'. Smith sees deep space as 'quintessentially' social space; as physical extent geographs and discourses traverse the deep spaces but none of them assume a transcendental status as a privileged representation of the 'reality beyond', the product of human signification practices circulate across the deep space as mere things among things.

If one acknowledges the fact that everyday life is discursive just like the practices of statecraft, and that popular geographs can be just as geopolitical as are institutionally produced counterparts, the notion of deep spaces enables to recognize the different modalities of social action from which these geographs emanate. In discussing how the practices of everyday life is filled with propositional moments when the weak can turn to their own ends forces alien to them, de Certeau (1984) points out that such an endeavor takes the form, however, not of a discourse, but the decision itself, the act and manner in which the opportunity (to manipulate events) is "seized". The spaces discursively produced by the political and administrative elites are not necessarily resisted through an engagement in a quest for political discourse (centered around, for instance, national security, development issues, regionalism, cultural values etc).

The resistance may equally dwell in the countless instances of every day social life in concrete lived spaces, that is, in deep spaces which evade the formal geo political discourse built upon the abstract spaces of archives, surveys and statistics. However, before going to take case of popular tactics of everyday life as perfectly capable of bringing institutional projects to their own ends, one needs to investigate the production of political space as an endeavour seeking to colonize symbolisms pertinent to the life world. In this context it is required to explore the gap between the lived social space and institutionally produced representations-the distance from "deep space" to politics and administrative discourse which allows and bears within itself social power, as well as resistance to that power. The starting point for a critical analysis of this gap could be set in terms of Foucault's power/knowledge as well as de Certeau's tactics of resistance by focusing on the NEI.

The Foucauldian notion of power/knowledge comes to much help in order to explore the historical development by which a region like NEI, where provincial symbolisms have become a strategic element in regional are administrative reforms and thereby part of the official regional discourses built upon the institutional infrastructures of statistics, surveys and mappings. His thought comes into help in tracing structures of power/knowledge in order to show how the state's discourses have given rise to and reproduced what Foucault (1991) has called governmentality; how state's development into a modern territorial system of power in fact also required and produced symbolic discursive territoriality and how the logistics of state activities, concrete practices and material operations weaved seams of knowledge that have symbolized and rationalized its practices of truth.

However, this theoretical framework needs to be broadened in the light of 'new regional geography', which conceives region as social construct (Murphy, 1991; Passi, 1991; Entrikin, 1994; Thrift; 1994). Socially constructed regions are not merely empirical units or containers of social processes, but social and symbolic processes interconnected with regional formation (Thrift, 1983; Passi, 1986a; Urry, 1987; Hakili, 1994a). In the framework of new regional geography regions have been conceptualized as symbolic processes integral to the situated social processes being studied. Thus instead of being immutable, regions are humanly produced and subjects to change as they are continuously reinterpreted and reproduced (Johnston, 1991;Passi, 1991,Taylor, 1991).

To understand the material embeddedness of deep space, Michel Foucault's ideas of power/knowledge offers relatively little insight. In this respect Lefebvre comes to help, as his notion of abstract space is useful in this context. Lefebvre's insistence upon the production of space as inherent to the processes of modernization, economic as well as governmental and his sense of the spatial embeddedness of power and knowledge provide critical arguments for a balanced analysis of territoriality and help intensifying its reflections on the 'concrete' or the 'material' dimensions of the social world. Another thinkers Pierre Bourdieu whose theoretical positions regarding political and human agency could perhaps be located somewhere in the middle between Foucault and Lefebvre. Bourdieu provides the key for the social dynamics and agency within the institutional fields of power. His ideas help in explicating the foundation upon which the symbolic of power of the state and communities rests, as well as the turning of the *savoir* of region into a taken-for-granted knowledge of provinces/territories.

State, Power and Discursive Practices of Territories/Provinces

It has been accepted that knowledge of society is not politically innocent. It is two-way avenue running back and forth in our social life. Research on ideology, imagery and discourses has shown that knowledge of society does not reflect 'reality-as-it-is', rather it is both conditioned by society and in its social construction. Furthermore, knowledge always represents a particular point of view highlighting certain features of social world while eclipsing others. Different perspectives of knowledge imply unmentioned preconditions, conditions, and practical and historical context, which enable and regulate the representation of social space (Bensman and Lilifeled, 1973; Agnew, 1987;Driver, 1992).

The focus here is on a particularly powerful and enduring perspective that is embedded in the political and administrative practices of the state. With reference to this one needs to outline history of state as the centre of production of knowledge of society.

The ubiquity of territoriality whether socially expressed in administrative or property relations, is markedly a characteristic of modern societies (Mann, 1984,2001; Ruggie, 1993; Hakli, 1994a). The pre-modern structures of administrative power lacked efficient (technological) means for integrating far-flung territories of 'heterogeneity'.

By contrast the modern state is clearly is a demarcated field of interacting with a far reaching functional division of labour between politico administrative 'systems' and the civil society (Soja, 1997;

Williams and Smith, 1983; Sack, 1986). The increasing interest of territoriality as a principle of politico-administrative practice was closely associated with new needs and technologies to coordinate people, things and activities into common events. This new field of societal intervention was both spatially larger than the traditional communities and reached 'deeper' into the civil society than the pre-modern state (Mann, 1984; Dandekar, 1990).

The increasing role of states as contexts of discourse was intimately associated with new rational ways of governing society. Rational government came to require a new empirical knowledge of society and rested on saviors no longer attached to the territory as an administrative realm, but rather to the multiple relations within the population and territory (Foucault, 1990:101). This new development is marked by the consolidation of the "perspectives of knowledge' i.e. discursive structures and limits of knowledge of the social world stemming from political and administrative interests of the state and is based on the absolute distinction between external reality and representation (or between the social world of matter and the conceptual orders, structures and laws which the political practical sought to know and visualize) (Mitchell, 1998; Rabinow, 1989). A map both as a metaphor and representation exemplifies well this mode of knowing (Harley, 1998,O` Tuathail, 1994a).

The metaphors of vision are particular apt here because it was largely through new visualizing devices and techniques the states have better hold of their territories and the societies 'within them' (Latour, 1986; Revel, 1991). The rise of knowledge to a strategic tool for rational government gave impetus to the proliferation of maps and statistical data that assumed new function and meaning as the new material of policy making (Porter, 1986; Foucault, 1991; Hacking, 1991). It is on this visualizing foundation that the centered discourse on social space began to grow.

The fact that states have become significant centers of symbolic power in modern societies is not without consequences. Many authors have pointed out that much of the social scientific knowledge is discursively related to the state (Giddens, 1985;Marricas, 1987; Withrock et al., 1989). This intertwinement is based on a shared (non) perspective from which the social world is viewed and portrayed. Among the recurring discursive limits implied by the perspective of power are the conception of 'society' as territorially confined, unit usually the nation-state, conception of space as the dead container of social relations, and conceptions of knowledge as an impartial mirror-image reality (Wagner, 1989, 1990; Harley, 1989a; Agnew, 1993).

Whether produced within the academics or bureaucracy, official discourses have the important function of providing policy-making with legitimate representation and categories of the social world (Bourdieu, 1989). They must sort out and ignore various different allegedly more 'subjective' view points arising from the 'civil society' in order to make space for an objective, universal one. Hence, the perspective of power presents itself as a non-perspective and an objective, universal and important ground of knowledge.

North-East India: the Colonial Geography of Knowledge

Region is a category commonly denoting a portion of earth's surfaces, a community of people or social relations across a given area none of which can be perceived directly. Scientific or governmental observation of regions is possible only by means of visualizing devices like statistics and maps. Knowledge based on observation of regions and territories are, thus, discursive construction, which rely on and presupposes a solid institutional foundation. This alone makes their relation to the state's discursive practices most intimate.

In NEI the foundation for the observation of region was laid in project of mapping by the colonizers, which are broadly understood in terms of centralized and systematic collection of empirical knowledge of society. A classic example of this can found in the nature of colonial intervention in the Naga Hills between 1840-80.The colonial writings of this period tried to analyze the Naga society, which were part of the overall British attempt at territorial consolidation in the Naga Hills (Misra, 1998). Central to the process of locating and extending the territoriality of the colonial state in the Naga Hills was a change in the ethnographic form of the writings, with its increasing concentration on mapping the territorial identification of reified tribes. While enabling the state to identify its territorial boundaries within a larger, stable, geographical context, maps furthered the process of rendering visible the subjects of colonization (ibid). The earliest attempt at concretizing the territorial imperatives of the colonial state in the Naga Hills was the map plotted during the expedition of Captain Butler in 1846. A J Moffat Mills in1853 in his report on the province of Assam writes:

Mr. Thornton who accompanied the expedition, surveyed the route traversed and plotted off on a large scale, a most valuable map of the greatest portions of Naga Hills attached to the district of Nowgong; the grand objects of the Naga expedition, the conciliation of the tribes and the acquirement of a more accurate knowledge of the country was therefore considered fully attained"(cited in Misra, 1998)

More significantly, the map was not necessarily a representation of the objective reality, but a model for, rather than a model of what it purported to represent. It was necessary for the administrative mechanism and for the troops to make up their claims. The discourse of mapping was the paradigm which both administrative and military operations worked within. In the colonial context of Naga Hills, the consistent redefining and demarcation of boundaries was reflective of such representative uses of the map. As early as 1842 proposals were put forward, for example by Lt.Bigge, for the demarcation of a boundary between the Angami Naga country and the British protectorate of Manipur, the objectives being clearly defined as "the separation of the Angami Nagas and the inferior tribes subject to their influence from the Nagas of Munnipore". Further the adoption of this boundary was to be the first step towards the permanent settlement of and acquisition of control over the Naga tribes making apparent the determination of the government to put down all aggression as the European officer placed in command would seek to establish control over the whole hill country. The demarcation of boundary between the Naga Hills and Manipur was completed only in 1873 but the intervening years were reflective of the role of the map in enforcing the colonization process. For example the Angami Hills were constituted as a separate district and boundary pillars were laid between the hills and plains below, all of which contributed towards the extension of colonial hegemony in the area.

That the processes of surveying and mapping were central to the colonial discourse is also evident in the often explicit political objectives that were assigned to them. The advocation of what was termed as gradual and systematic prosecution of the survey of the hills was not to be limited to "purposes of exploration but for a continuation of the political occupation of the hills"(Mackenzie, 1884 cited in Misra, 1998). Thus the Grange's expedition in 1938 meted out deterrent punishment to Angami Nagas accused of killing British subjects, "democratizing thereby that the English had the power of bringing to book even the strongest confederacy of the Nagas (cited in Misra, 1998).

Beside the Naga case another important example can be forwarded as an example of discursive practices of provinces i.e. the formation of the province of Assam in the colonial period. When the Ahom Kingdom passed into British hands, it was the first time in history that Assamese heartland became politically incorporated into a pan-Indian imperial formation (Baruah, 1999) in 1826 through signing the Yandabo Treaty. Before it became a colonial province there were two large political formations in the region i.e. the Koch Kingdom which encompassed eastern Assam and significant parts of northern Bengal that now form the part of Bangladesh and the Indian state of West Bengal and Ahom Kingdom located in the extreme northeastern corner of subcontinent. Assam as a colonial province –a chief commissionership was formed in 1874. The primary goal of making Assam into a new administrative entity was to find an inexpensive and effective way to administer the area; considerations of historical continuity or cultural continuity were not in the minds of the colonial officials (ibid). The consolidation of colonial power in the province of Assam was carried out through inclusion and exclusion of newer areas. Facts about this are scattered in the colonial writings and historiography. An administrative report said as-

> *it is proposed to add Goalparah [Goalpara] and the Garo Hills on the West, and Sylhet and Cachar on the south, with Munnipore [Manipur] on the southeast ...the details connected with the transfer are still under consideration.*

One of the earliest proposal considered was to include the Western Duars and the districts of Koch Bihar, Jalpaiguri and Darjeeling. Another proposal was to include Chittagong. The Western Duars, Koch Bihar, Jalpaiguri and Darjeeling today are in the districts of West Bengal and Bangladesh. The Lieutenant Governor of Bengal, Sir George Campbell, was obsessed with the idea of political boundaries of new unit of Assam coinciding with the natural boundary line drawn up by the Meghna and the Surma. Following this the decision to bring Sylhet was taken in which not only separated the Bengali –speaking on either side of the Meghna but also engendered the rivalry between two valleys of the Brahmaputra and Surma which has continued with occasional breaks till modern time. A number of territories annexed to the British empire in subsequent years were incorporated into Assam: notably the country of the *Lhota Nagas* 1875, that of the *Angami Nagas* in 1878-80 and of the *Ao Nagas* in 1889, and that of the *Lushais* (Mizo)-conquered between 1871 and 1889 but constituted into a district of Assam in 1898. For a brief period proposal for the inclusion of Chittagong and Decca was also considered to reduce the cost of transportation and to develop Chittagong as an outlet to the sea for tea. The colonial administration did succeed to combine Assam and Eastern Bengal-the present day Bangladesh into a single province but for a brief time. The province of East Bengal and Assam proved to be short-lived, and in 1912 Assam reverted to its former status as chief commissionership and to its former boundaries that included Sylhet. Assam was upgraded into the Government of India Act. of December 1919.

Given the circumstances of the formation of the British province of Assam, the boundaries for the very reason do not coincide with those of the pre-colonial Assam in a political, cultural or economic sense. The decision on Assam's boundaries was based on consideration of administrative convenience and on the whims of the colonial administrators. Certain areas were not historically part of Assam became part of colonial Assam, whether other areas that were a part of Assam did not form the Colonial Assam.

The Rise of Nation-State and the Discursive Practices of Regions

The 19th century witnessed an epistemic break as 'region's were no longer considered tied merely to the praxis of administration but could also be constructed in terms of scientific discourses and political trends and aspirations of given time. In fact, 'Regions' became part of the politics of representation. It became increasingly differentiated with 'landscape', which implied a perspectivist connotation as a way of seeing from a particular vantage point. 'Region' became a discursive product that has tended to deny due particularity in the relations between the viewer and the viewed. As a space of observation, analysis and reflection it claims to represent all perspectives, and thus resonates the discourses of modern governmentality. In this sense in the course of 19th century 'region' overlapped with, but also partly replaced 'landscape' as a way of seeing of the powerful classes, which via state supported professional systems, more intimately became attached with the bureaucracy than previously before. This was particularly the case of the state-centered societies (Collins, 1990; Kentinnen, 1991).

With the formation of Nation-state, 'region' came to signify only a province/administrative blocks in the eyes of the State in terms of certain linguistic/cultural traits. In a democratic centralized polity of India nowhere the term 'region' incorporated things like its unique history, cultural and social formations. It came to be identified with a politico-administrative unit, whose continued survival is dictated by the power matrix in which it is located. In short, the 'region' is referred to simply as an ecological niche as seen by the powers that be-near to the centre and or far-but also represents a probable near-homogeneity of the people living there with some degree of autonomy under the centralized nation-state system. Post-colonial exigencies and cultures determine the term, thereby implying that such spaces are unchangeable or immune to change.

The 'Committee' institution was one of the features inherited by the post-colonial Indian State as a legacy of the colonial politico-administrative system. The committees remained as more or less temporary bodies of experts appointed by the state and central govt. to give guidance in particularly demanding questions. However, in terms of their function these were not only practical but also discursive. Committees were asked for establishing what is real and what forms the point of view of the government in power. Their task was to reduce uncertainty and diversity with regard to categories and perceptions of the social world and thereby enable the politico- administrative practice of the State usually in the fields that were new to it (Burton and Carlen, 1979; Bourdieu, 1989:22).

When the question of regional administration surfaced in the Indian politico-administrative discourse the task was given to Committees to attempt the definition and demarcation of a new political space within the Indian polity. After Independence the task of demarcation of territories was given to the State Reorganization Committee (SRC). The committee took linguistic provinces as the basis of this reorganization. However, in the case of NEI the reorganization of the region on the basis of language posed immense problem, as there are no areas in the region where a single language is generally accepted as the local language. The notion of legitimization of state on the basis language became potentially divisive in a multi- ethnic and multi-lingual setting like the NEI. In the absence of common single language the demand for statehood were mostly based on mobilization of symbols other than language as it happened in the Indian mainland. The demand for a 'hill state' for instance attempted to mobilize the sentiments of hill people against the plainsmen. What eventually emerged as a result of this demand was not a single hill state, but a number of mini states, none of which are linguistically homogenous. Many of them have English as their official language.

The first prime minister of independent India, Pt. Jawaharlal Nehru had a vision of NEI in which the tribals would be allowed to develop according to their own genius and Assam would be a great centre of contact between the civilization of India and China. Against this background, the Constituent Assembly, which in turn constituted a sub-committee, styled as the North-East Frontier (Assam) Tribal and Excluded Areas Sub-Committee. The Committee recommended that (1) the Khasi and Jaintia Hills District (excluding Shillong town), the Garo Hills Districts, the Lushai Hills District, the North Cachar Hills and the Mikir Hills excluding certain plains areas to be made autonomous districts with wide ranging powers vested in the District Councils for the administration and development of these areas ;(2) the Sadiya and Balipara Frontier Tracts, the Tirap Frontier Tract and the Naga Tribal Areas to be made autonomous areas and the responsibility for their all-round administration and development to be vested on the Governor of Assam; and (3)the plains tribals of Assam should be recognized as a minority and be entitled to all privileges of a minority, including representations in legislatures and in the services and their land to be protected. All these recommendations were accepted and provisions were made in the Constitution and the laws framed thereafter, Manipur and Tripura retained their individual identities in the new constitutional set up.

Meanwhile the central government's idea of District Council to be set up met with a disaster in the Naga Hills as the *Nagas* boycotted the elections to it due to suspicions in the tribal mind regarding their identity and economic independence. Another Commission headed by H.V. Pataskar was set up to look into the demands of the Hill leaders in 1965 also met the similar fate as the recommendation of the Commission did not satisfy anyone except Assam. On 11th September 1968, the establishment of an autonomous State of Meghalaya within Assam was announced with the proviso that pubic order and the police would remain with Assam, along with certain financial and taxation matters. However, the experiment was short lived. It failed to satisfy the tribal elites of Meghalaya. Finally with the passing of the North-Eastern Areas (Reorganization) Bill in 1971 the NEI came to have seven political units (seven sisters) and nascent regional planning authority –the North Eastern Council (N.E.C).

The N.E.C as a spatial planning body carried out the regional planning practices through regionalization on the basis of different criteria. With its highly technological and bureaucratic approach the basis for integrated planning for the NEI region became faulty. For example the N.E.C regards the seven administrative units of NEI as the sub-regions of the North-Eastern macro region. But these states and union territories are far from homogenous either from the geographer's point of view or from that of an economist. The N.E.C fails to recognize adequately the intra-regional, inter-state heterogeneity arising out of difference in physiography, demographic characteristics, inaccessibility and distance from the nodal point of the region. The N.E.C's integral agricultural programme makes broad distinctions between the hills and the plains and also makes passing reference to watershed development. But all hills are not alike and all valleys cannot be similarly treated (Bhattacharjee, 1985).

From the above discussion one can conclude that the governmental discourse grounded in the abstract space of institutional strategies has logic of its own which does not grasp the everyday lived world even when the 'perspective of power' is made to conflate with the vernacular ones. The discursive of practices of 'State' of transformation of territories/provinces instead of bringing about a politico-administrative system of a 'more humane scale and quality', the conflation of governmental conception of political space and the popular symbolisms of provinces only defines the moment of colonization of the latter by the former. The official discourse of one-dimensional (non) perspective of power entails a homogenizing gaze with the potential to colonize the multidimensional and heterogeneous symbolisms of provinces embedded in everyday lives. The official discourse is a representing 'arbitrary and artificiality' of regions from the above while the discourses of everyday life emerging out of 'deep space' comes from below. The demand for 'autonomous provinces' in the case of NEI comes from liberal idea of civil society embedded in the 'deep space'. The official discourses the committee reports reduces the discourses emerging out of 'deep space' into geometric, homogenous, one dimensional plane. However, one will be mistaken if one considers the present development as a mark of the victory of the lived spaces or the popular symbolisms of various autonomous regions.

The Political Economy of Space in North-East India

According to Lefebvre social space is the location of the reproduction of relations of production and 'society' in all its complexity. To him (social) space is a product implying that every society with all its sub variants produces space of its own. However, space is not only a product of spatialising but also a product of medium. This ontological transformation of space emerges from his inspiration from Hegel, Marx and Engels. Lefebvre enlarges the narrower industrial sense (production of products, commodities) to include the production of spatialised meanings and other codings of the social environment. In doing so he presupposes that Marx's concept of commodity production represents a model by which the multiple dualisms of his analysis of space can best be accommodated. However, unlike other commodities or products, space has both a material reality that enables it to constrain other formal commodities and their social relations. It continually recreates or reproduces the social relations of its production. Space has the property of being materialized by specific social processes to act upon. It is, therefore, simultaneously material object or product, the medium of social relations, and the reproducer of material objects and social relations. In this manner Lefebvre grounds the multi-faceted nature of the interrelations between society and its space in a dialectical framework, transforming Marx's original ontological categories by the addition of spatial dimensions (Shields, 1999). For Lefebvre's Marx, social space is simultaneously a means of production as land and part of the social forces of production as space. In addition space is an instrument and an element of struggle.

An exploration in production and reproduction of space in NEI can take a cue from the above framework as it can better explain the multifarious interrelationship between societies and space in heterogeneous setting like the NEI. In the similar light one needs an understanding of the spatial location and distribution of relations of production both at the structural level and superstructural level in order to understand the production and reproduction of social space in NEI.

Relations of Production and Space

In the case of NEI space is structured by heterogeneous and context sensitive modes of production and in a sense space functions as medium of social relations and gets limited by reproduction. Space is ordered and organized in a manner that can sustain a certain mode of production and vice a versa. But the crucial matter is that space differs from a category like 'relations of production' is that it is not just a material construct but it is an experiential and lived notion. Space therefore is not only stands for relations of production but it produces a basis for organizing relations of production within that given form of society. This shows how space itself it produced within relations of production by its very nature, which is social. The social space by the same account is a space of production, which gets enmeshed into space that is produced. But the produced space appears as an experience of a certain mode of living and thereby becomes a part of social practices. In the case of NEI, production of space remains a part of heterogeneity of modes of production, which gets located in different spatial positions. In other words, heterogeneity is spatial such that it establishes a relationship between different modes of production and stretches through the entirety of the produced space.

The social and cultural production of space, the social relations of production as shaped by modes production acts as a sources of construing space as 'place', location and habitat etc. In other words space acquires a distinct characteristics only through situating itself within modes of production. Such a situation of space simultaneously organizes the productive activities manifested in the forms of production and then gets limited by socially constructed narratives and signifiers of community and life. The spatial distribution of modes of production and the ways in which it is culturally mediated constitute the production of space in NEI. The production of space and spaces of production are both mediated by social and cultural conditions of production. The location of communities in space and evolution of a sense of belonging give rise to processes of mapping the place into space and reproducing the mapped space in an orderly fashion. The notion of landscape signifies an association between modes of production and belonging to designated space. The actual uses and experiences of space centers around the sense of mode of production and belonging to the space. Belonging to the space is a product of the practice of production as disjunction between the two would make unfamiliar, as social forces produce space and it is a social product. So the distinct characteristics of space are manifested through inalienable ties with space. Therefore production of space as an activity of production cannot overcome the limits put by belonging to a case which itself is determined by a historical mode of production. Such a determination of space by the mode of production and vice versa provides the basis for spatializing modes of production of spaces to which modes of production can belong to.

Modes of Production and Space

In the case of NEI modes of production is embedded and emplaced in different locales. The spatiality of social and economic relations in a particular locale characterizes the mode of production. It is the local milieu, which is fundamental to the production of space in NEI. The three delineated modes of production i.e. Domestic, Intermediary and Capitalistic modes of production have emerged historically through social and economic practices of different locales (see Table no. 5).

The Domestic modes of production is mainly characterized by economic activities like hunting and gathering, shifting cultivation etc. and these emerged from the interaction of ethnic groups in the hills and the stretches of lowland. Here *Jhumming* is the mode of agriculture and it is supplemented by other activities like gathering of forest products, fishing and weaving. The community owns means of productions and there is provision of communitarian share of labour also. In the low stretches of hills and terraces and lowlands wet rice is cultivated. Mostly the families consume surplus and some portion of it is sold to the middlemen.

The Intermediary Modes of Production is characterized by a 'mercantile economy' run on monopoly of petty traders. It not only includes commercial agriculture but also petty trade. This mode of production historically emerged in the sub-montanne areas of the foothill and *duars* of the NEI region where most of the big *hats* (fairs) are located. These areas have a strategic advantage as being in sub-montanne location formed by common boundaries with both hills and valleys.

The Capitalist Modes of Production operates mostly in the urban centers of NEI. These urban centers have been the colonial sites of accumulations well connected through the roadways and railways where most of the extractive industries are located. It also encompasses the administrative cities and centers of education once developed by the colonial power.

These three modes of production is the outcome of the mutual interaction between different spaces in the locale. The intermediary mode of production is a classic example of how spaces are extended

Table No. 5
Interrelationship Between Modes of Production and Space

Modes of Production	Domestic	Intermediary	Capitalistic
Locale	• Hills •Terraces and Stretches of Lowlands • Valleys • Peripheral Rural Townships	• Sub-montanne Areas •Foothills • Duars	• Industrial and Administrative Cities having colonial roots • New Urban Agglomerations
Modes of Social and Economic Practices	• Hunting & Gathering • Jhumming • Cultivation of Wet Rice -Horticulture •Commercial trade in fish and forest products • Petty Commercial Activities like contract jobs, money lending etc.	• Settled Agriculture • Cultivation of Cash Crops	• Resource Based Industries like oil, tea and plywood • Service Sector and Welfare State
Class	Rural Petty Bourgeoisie	Regional Bourgeoisie	Middle and Elite Class
Economy	Homestead	Mercantile	Under-developed Capitalistic

through dominant modes of production which subsumes modes of production that are less dominant. It emerged in NEI during the colonial intervention in the trade in the foothills, which had been traditionally the place for exchange between the highlanders and the plainsman and where most of the big *hats* (fairs) are located. It is where the dominant modes of production like the capitalist modes of production came in touch with the domestic modes of production. From the very beginning the capitalist modes of production tried to pull down all the local barriers to commerce, as it was pertinent on the part of the colonizers to transfer the economic resource of periphery to the metropolitan centers of production. However, in the absence of a local professional commercial class who could seek collaboration and mediate between invasive capitalism and the indigenous homestead economy it introduced an intermediary class mostly *of Marwaris* who were operating in Assam as agents of British trading houses in Calcutta. The colonizers wanted the tribes to be economically more dependent on trade with the plainsman in order to exert pressure on them to concede to the colonial interests and thus to extend their hegemony in the region (Sikadar, 1982). However, restricted pattern mainly based on (monopoly and unequal exchange) of trade could not initiate any structural change in the economy and hence ruled out the possibility of the emergence of a new 'comprador class' (ibid). The introduction of 'cash money' played an important role in breaking up of the traditional system of exchange.

After independence the process moved further and the village in the foothills began to reap benefits of government sponsored agricultural programmes along with the other opportunities. Among certain tribes the response has been quick and than adopted commercial agriculture and contract jobs in a big way. Hence, this intermediary space is conditioned by the space of exchange between local sellers and the buyers located within the network of market forces. Such an exchange converts the living space of exchange into 'space of exchanged' within the lived space. Therefore, in the intermediary mode of production the space is captured by an exchange relationship, which turns it into others' space that emerges out of this space of location. Intermediary mode of production, therefore shows how production as an activity reorganizes space, rather alters it characteristics by producing a space of difference than the familiar lived space. This difference in space gets mediated by the culture and market, thereby foregrounding the produced space over the space of the production.

In the capitalist modes of production the space of NEI as whole acts as an economic space subsumed within the national economy and emerged as a market for finished products, an extension of national space over and above its local characteristics. In conjunction between all the three production the spaces of NEI assumed modes of double role of being what it is and an intension, a habitat as well as an extension of a larger national space. Going by its intension the space constitutes production and organizes itself around the cultural and social conditions of production. Such an intension remains self-content within the domestic and the intermediary modes of production, as in both the modes of production does not substantially alters the space beyond the sense of place or location. Production of space in this case is limited by belonging to place and space is confined and circumscribed within the place itself. Alteration of space in intermediary modes of production alters the space within the place and thereby limit the production of space by greater role of the 'local' factors. In both these modes, social construction of space is guided by place oriented social beings and captured by sustenance of modes of production, which grounds space in place. Of course, such a grounding does not obliterate differential spaces within the locale and there is no strict correspondence between space and place, rather a contradiction within modes of production prevent an alternative space to emerge from existing social relations of production.

The Self, the Other and the Poetics of Space

According Harvey (1989) spatial practices 'take their meanings under specific social relations of class, gender, community, ethnicity or race and get "used up" or "worked over" in the course of social action. Referring to Lefebvre, Harvey goes on to note that tension and conflict arise within society over the uses of space for individual and social purposes and the domination of space by the state and other forms of class and power. This conflict can give rise to social movements whose aim is to liberate space by resisting the processes of domination. Such conflicts are grounded in particular places, since place is the arena where social structure and social relations intersect, giving rise to relations of power, domination and resistant.

An exploration in the notions of identity reveals the fact that place is a critical source of group politico-territorial identity and the politics of signification is quite contradictory in terms of expression of resistance and domination. The construction and '*self*' and '*others*' is eventually geographical in nature because it bases critically on a presupposition that place and sense of place is a powerful source of group politico-territorial identity. However, this constitution may not be necessarily grounded on the locale. In other words, a sense of place being derived from local social worlds may also go beyond the locality (Pred, 1984; Agnew, 1993). Thus a sense of place is as much as a product of social processes on different scales, which are brought together and mediated through the cultural practices of specific locales.

Ethnic politics is radically different from the politics of identity, which is not grounded on homelands–the letter is often easily incorporated within a larger ideology of state nationalism (Baruah,1999). The politics of sub-nationalism premised on poetics about homeland and its people. If nations and nationalities are 'imagined communities', it is a poetics that transfer the 'geography' of an area into a primal 'home-like' or 'sacred space' and transforms the people into a collectivity with imagined ties of shared origins and kinships (ibid). In similar lines Harvey (1993) argues that placed-bound identities when conflated with race and ethnicity produce a reactionary exclusionary politics. He evokes the Heideggarian notion of 'dwelling' to explain how this desire can lead to parochial and aggressive claims over territory and identity. He argues that there is a deep-rooted crisis of homeliness within the modern world where people have lost their roots, their connection to homeland and their capacity to 'dwell'.

The NEI has been witnessing heightened forms of separatism and distancing with relations with the others is tending to occupy a central place in the politics of sub-nationalism in NEI. The geographies of dissent is a testimony to the signification of place construction as dominant feature of contemporary life world of NEI. In the case of NEI place construction is governed and regulated by critical geographical markers of Hills vs. Plains, Peripheries vs. Market and Administrative centers, Rural vs. Urban which has already occupied the common sense division of space. Such common sense markers assume constructionist metaphors like territories, homeland, terrain (as the markers of the 'self'), as well as outside markers like place names and reference to other people (e.g. *dakars*, *bhais*, *bhatias*, *ujani*, *charua* etc.) such spaces which are marked and signified by a cultural location, site of production relations to the immediate spaces with which it interacts. The denigration of 'other's places ensemble the means to assert the viability and incipient power of one's own place. The contest over images and counter-images of place is an area in which is cultural politics of place construction is played out dialectically across material, representational and symbolic activities which find their hallmark in the way in which communities invest in places and thereby empower collectively by virtue of that investment.

The post-colonial space in NEI is occupied with conflicting tensions that arise when the 'self' comes to face with the 'other' who is considered as a stranger who comes uninvited and invades the life-world of the indigenous population. This is a constant struggle as Derridian deconstruction shows, otherness has been appropriated by logocentrism whereby the 'other' is mastered and its alterity reduced. Proximity to the stranger also reveals a veiled intimacy between the stranger and the subjectivity and the social, mainly brought about by imaginary constructions of the 'other' and its potential threat. The heterogeneity of the setting in a region like NEI produces a gamut of experiences embracing the tribal, the non-tribal and the migrant living in different locales. The separatist and ethnic movements in the region bases itself on the geographical markers in defining the 'self' and the 'other' through cultural mediations. A classic example is the Assam Movement, in which various geographical metaphors (e.g. the perception of the territory of Assam imbued with the signification of the body of mother, the river *Brahmaputra*) were used mostly drawn from the songs of popular singer Bhupen Hazarika. Similarly, secessionist demand for separate homelands also emerges on the markers drawn from the lived space of the communities (like the demand for a Greater Nagaland, the demand for a separate Bodoland). The '*other*' (mostly the migrant communities) is conceived as a cause for the 'imagined theft of pleasure' and it becomes unbearable as it acts as a remainder of the impossibility of one's own enjoyment. The spatial configuration of everyday life is fused with complex patterns of difference with the arrival of the stranger that is so compelling. Therefore, the politics of place construction within the sub-nationalism can become highly reactive and exclusionary, whereby the synthesis of nearness and remoteness produces a threatening form.

North-East India: A Critical Geographical Praxis

Underdevelopment is characterized by over accumulation of capital within some particular geographical area coupled with unequal insertion of different territories and social formations into the fold of the national capital. Development process acts as a medium for the geographical reorderings and restructuration of the space as necessary foundation for capitalist accumulation. It leads to perpetual production, reproduction and sustenance of geographical difference in ways of life, standards of living, resource uses, and relations to environment and cultural political forms at different scales (Harvey, 2000). Throughout history capitalism has been found to build and rebuild the geography of regions and countries in its own image giving rise to distinct social and economic landscapes, with a produced space of transport and communications, of infrastructure and territorial organization in order to facilitate capital accumulation. The discourse of development uses spaces as it ontologically grounds production of space and therefore, gives rise to a discourse about material production, which further gives rise to signification of economic and cultural practices.

In the sphere of production different relations of production gives rise to different modes of development. For example in the case of NEI the domestic modes of production gives rise to self-reliant modes of development whereas the intermediary and capitalistic modes of production gives rise to dependent modes development. These different modes of development get intertwined in space at different scales. The development process suppresses and represses the space of production at different scales. The capitalist modes of production envelop both the space of the domestic and the intermediary modes of production. It extends its hegemony through suppressing the productive capacities of the domestic modes of production and at the same time flexibilizing the space of the domestic for opening the gateway for the flow of the commodities from the centre. Therefore, by suppressing the basic modes of production at one scale and on other scale through the introduction of market and monetization of production relations it creates an uneven geographical development, which leads to intensification of spatial and social inequalities.

The uneven geographical development is created by targeting the space of the domestic modes of production in the peripheries. The modernization process comes as a handy tool in this process. The government's initiation of permanent settlement and private property in the tribal belt is a step towards it. The introduction of market in the peripheries and increasing commodification have led the traditional cultivators loosing his stake in fruits of development as he no longer can compete with the commercial production. For example the *Karbis* in the district Karbi Anglong Hills of Assam led a migratory life because of shifting cultivation. The location of a *Karbi* village has never been a true geographical unit, fixed on the landscape. Traditionally the *Karbis* used to practice *Jhumming* in harmony with the local ecology. However, the official strategy of enhancing the *Jhum* holding productivity through extension service and modern technology led increased pressure on the local environment which led to deforestation and loss of soil fertility and grossly affected the productivity of the tribal cultivators. The erosion of means of production of the traditional farmers led to increase dependency on others. As a result the *Karbis* started hiring the lands for various kinds of sharecropping locally known as *Paikas, Sukti Bandhak, Khoi Bandhak* with the non-tribals against payments in cash and or kinds for periods ranging from one to five years. Once a tribal enters into such a system he hardly ever comes out which leads to land alienation.

The maldistribution in the material base provides the space for articulation of resistance. The material conditions of the groups in the region engaged in symbolic politics of recognition mirror the conditions of a colonial hinterland at the periphery of political and economic decision-making. The unevenness of development provides the basis for drawing political and ethnic boundaries, which is culturally mediated. It is the regional bourgeoisie, the elites of the dominant class and the new tribal elites rather than the subalterns that take active participation in drawing such exclusive boundaries. For example in the case of two autonomous districts of Karbi Anglong and the North Cachar Hills enjoyed a special status since the days of the Government Of India Act of 1935 which continued to remain part of Assam. Although they have been politically and administratively part of Assam but they have never viewed themselves as part of Assam. A section of the political leadership of the two autonomous districts tried to make common cause with the other autonomous districts that eventually became the state of Meghalaya in 1960s. The All Party Hill Leaders Conference (APHLC), which spearheaded the agitation in the Khasi and Jaintia Hills and the Garo Hills could not prevail upon (then) Mikir and North Cachar Hills district to throw in their lot as the Karbi people were suspicious of the leadership of the APHLC and being one of the more 'Assamised'of the several tribes of the state. However, the same people who resisted the blandishments of APHLC are now seeking greater autonomy than that has been provided under the Sixth Schedule of the Constitution which clearly shows the emergence and consolidation of more articulate political elites within the Karbi society.

Similarly, the All Bodo Student's Union, Upendra Brahma faction (ABSU-UB) seeking initially the constitution of virtually the whole of the north bank of the river Brahmaputra into a union territory with additional safeguards for the tribal people on the south bank of river Brahmaputra and for the Bodo Kachari people in Karbi Anglong (which was later upgraded as the greater 'Bodoland') district points out a similar story. The agitation for a separate Bodoland has been marked by considerable violence. Aside the intrastate disputes there are many inter-state boundary disputes in the region. For example the boundary dispute between the Assam and Nagaland has been more serious. There have been also incidents between Assam and Arunachal, and Assam and Meghalaya. Claims for the transfer of Naga inhabited areas of Manipur to Nagaland and of the areas inhabited by Kuki-Chin group of tribes to Mizoram have been made in the in the past. To both these claims the Meities are firmly opposed. Mizoram has also made claims for transfer of its area of Assam and Tripura, and Tripura and Assam are resolutely opposed to these claims.

The foregoing account gives an example how boundaries are drawn to maintain and manage underdevelopment. According to David Harvey (2000), the changing case of territorialization clearly shows that there is nothing 'natural' about political boundaries even if natural features have played some kind of role in their definition. Territorialization is, in the end, an outcome of political struggle and decision made in a context of technological and political-economic conditions. In the case of NEI territorialization and de-territorialization have become a geographical means in the hands of regional elites and the newly formed tribal elites by which they try to by-pass and undermine from outside and subvert from inside place bound feudal powers. In NEI boundaries have been drawn to maintain and manage underdevelopment, which serves the interests of particular class. It has been always the regional tribal and the national elites rather than the subalterns who are involved in the demarcation of boundaries. By means of this the elites have been trying to convert the state into the executive of its own ambition. And, once in power, the bourgeoisie continued to pursue the mission in part via both external and internal geographical transformation. The boundaries act as the primary symbolic marker for underdevelopment and if one takes a bottom up approach one can see how boundaries change only if one moves from underdevelopment to development (for example if one moves from a peripheral place like Hajo to Guwahati and not the other way round). The everyday life of the tribal and the non-tribals doesn't the follow the demarcation of boundaries as these communities have been interacting with each other since time immemorial. The tribal locale forms a vast untapped resource base, which lures the capital to make it the global site for aid and development. It seems capital looks backwards to the backyards in search of space for creation of uneven geographical development bypassing center-periphery mode of development.

Finally, for critical geography of knowledge production, it is the location that plays the role of mediating capacitates of the State, which brings development. In this case communities living in the peripheries become the subjects of dominant geography of knowledge production as the geographical practices like map making, boundary demarcation have served particular interests in favour of the capital. As discussed earlier the tribal population became the target of such practices. There has been a continuation of the same practices till today if one considers the examples discussed in this particular section. Such discourses goes parallel with the discourse of the dominant class as it fulfills the aspiration of the same .So, production of spaces of underdevelopment is essential to governmentality.

4

Underdevelopment and its Cultural Implications in North-East India

Background

This chapter seeks to examine how the simultaneous coexistence of contradicting modes of production engaged in a relationship of dominance and dependency affect the specific relations of production that go into structuring the cultural identities of NEI. In particular how an ontological structuring of cultural identities affect distinct forms of political identities that emerge as a sum total of economic and social relations of production as articulated in the public sphere (Roy Burman, 1989). Further, how identities bear categories of development such as tribal, non-tribal or nationality etc. by generally coexisting in a plane of civil society and contained within the contours of politics. How a multiplicity of factors of social, cultural and economic realms affect the construction of cultural identity within the structural relations of Political Economy (Adorno, 1990) and how it negotiates the heterogeneous field of forces to stabilize itself. Does it remain self-same or produces itself in difference to itself? Such questions do arise in the field of inquiry that on the one hand hypothesizes the level of development in socioeconomic terms as the key factor in deciding the shape of identities, while on the other such development contributes to multiple possibilities of conflict, alliance and break ups between identities and the social classes involved in their making and unmaking. In the context of NEI inhabited by some 500 tribal groups and other larger identities, the field produces the challenge of indeterminacy beyond the fixed calculi of relations of production, while looked from inside relations of production fashion a stage of development that propels identities towards a resolution of the polyethnic and multinational ensemble into a determination of the structure and the agency.

The crucial question of the interrelationship between structure and agency becomes one of 'cultural politics', i.e., *how the signifying practices or ethnic markers of a community affect its identity and its relationship with 'others in a multicultural and polyethnic context'*? The question also relates the nature of contest between ethnic, tribal and communitarian identities with identities construed by the State to bring into focus how ethnic communities are positioned. Further this positioning is an act of claiming the identity vested on them which calls for a political positioning of their culture, so that it is not appropriated in the currents of domination.

Although the life-world of the ethnic communities are affected under modernity by the State, social identity and social relations of production, such affectation produces what is called the 'subject effect' upon the community. Such an effect is realized in the structure of the community that undergoes drastic changes such as emergence of elite and non-elite classes as poles within it. This has its disparaging effect of a ravage between the two classes in cultural terms, which signifies a new mode of legitimation and evaluation within the community. Even at a moment of revision of some of its tradition, the new criterion of value usually augured by the elites remain alien with respect to their culture and grope to find its grounds within the culture. One can call this situation as a kind of detribalization or decontextualization of tribal 'form of life' from within. Although it does not mean a wholesale merger with others radically different than them, but it opens up another way of signifying the already existing practices. This is also an effect of negotiating with an alien mode of production imposing itself through agencies of development. The utility and use of a large number of traditional tribal objects, starting from attire to musical instruments come into a newer strategic use to signify tribal life-world in the context of encountering an alien cultural practice. Therefore decontextualization does not uproot the identifying premises of tribal life, which are their cultural practices. Decontextualization brings out a moment of renewal bringing together radically new combinations of the old and the new within the cultural practices of tribal community. The question is whether the development process deconterxtualizes the tribal communities by introducing a kind of homogenization with the dominant.

But looking into this moment of decontextualization in the tribal life of NE-India one sees a reverse move of recalling of the tradition, because the newness of something calls forth grounding of tribal life in a new tradition. It re-grounds the tribal tradition in the upcoming and new tradition. Here comes a crucial dimension of positioning them as one among the multi-cultural identities with 'Indian' tradition, a task set out by the nationalist cultural politics. With an invigorated rise of ethnic consciousness, the rejection of a common assimilative cultural tradition by the tribals resists canonization of their culture by the dominant 'centre' of Indian culture. Contrarily, starting from within one's own tradition and remaining fully attached to it, the tribals of NE-India are negotiating their cultural tradition with others within the larger multi cultural fabric of Indian situation which has its basis right here and now.

Cultural politics of NE-Indian tribes resist the onslaught of nationalist-statist politics of cultural devaluation, canonization and homogenization by way of self-representation and maintenance of traditional community institutions. For example, a cult like *Doini-Polo, Seng Khasi* or celebration of *Gangngai* by *Rongmei Nagas* stand as a resistance to dominant processes of Hinduization or Christianization as such processes accompany opening of tribal social spaces to the spaces of market and state. It is in this sense; self-enclosed tribal communities need to be reevaluated from the perspective of giving them an independent recognition and freeing them permanently from the possibility of overt and covert cultural and economic domination. In a situation of substantial culture change, the tribals retain their signifying practices in a negotiating mode. The participation of Christian *Hmars* and *Lushais* in traditional festivities like *Butu khuong Lawm, Chalpou kut, Mim Kut* or *Chapchar Kut* bring back a renewed sense of tribal identity. Even though religious converts do not participate in rituals associated with such *Kuts*, the celebration takes a secular character. This internal secularization is also a part of cultural positioning of the tribe in a self-conscious acceptance of something 'better'. No Mizo can isolate herself from the almost two century influence of Christianity in bringing about a sense of modernity, but at the same time the continuance of some their signifying practices retain a sense of age old identity. Similarly, the division between *Seng Khasi* and *Christian Khasis* is not a water-tight division, as lots of *Khasi* practices explore the spaces 'in-between' and onto both the traditional and the new form of life. This aspect of positioning between the two modes of practice to negotiate the two enlarges the space of tribal identity in a mix between the indigenous and the endogenous elements. Such far reaching changes within the cultural identity demonstrates a self-conscious alteration of their identity and it will be interesting to find out whether relations of production act as a force of change or it resists change. It could be understood by taking into account the degree of difference that factors responsible for new developments produce and sustain the cultural identity without affecting the sense of specificity and distinction. In order to accomplish this it is necessary to identify those categories of Political Economy that play a significant role in driving this whole process to a direction of changes from within as well from without.

Cultural Economy and Modes of Development

These remarks begin the task of situating cultural production firmly within the domain of the social. They serve, too, as a prelude to the proposition that the cultural economy in capitalism is just another way of producing human culture, though it does not produce just any culture; on the contrary, the outputs of the modern cultural economy bear a determinate relationship to their social (capitalistic) conditions of production. It is in this relationship that a practice of economic production is culturally determined in such a way that it bears the mark of identity. Products of cultural economy agglomerate together in order to establish a chain of mutually fitting relations that bear a necessary coordinating function as they perform within the culture. Production in this sense becomes performances guided by the norms that govern the sum total of social relations within a culture.

Cultural Economy in the Context of NEI

Cultural Economy in the context of NEI remains at the grass root level productive activity by making use of resources in a skilled manner which follows small scale domestic supply of factors of production based on which an equitable distribution of utility is performed at the level of community. The community bases such a productive activity upon a primarily collective ownership over basic resources. Land, for example, the most basic of all other factor of production is collectively owned by most of the tribal communities. Apart from such factors of production, sharing of common products for various purposes of individual and social life extends the domestic production relation to maintain and sustain a form of life outside the pale of market, but enriched and guided by social relation (Bahadur, 2000). Further, these social relations sustain itself both materially as well as culturally by creating domains of meaning specific to various products, which are aesthetically produced to mark an immediate meaning from life. Hand-woven fabrics of various tribes, in fact any tribe of NEI mark a sphere of exclusive meaning by a play of colour and embroidery that will define an identity. In other words, social relations of production sustain itself in the sphere of the symbolic and aesthetic by assuming a kind of sublime that overcomes the vicissitudes of economic life.

Economic Relations as the Dominant Social Force

The domestic mode of production and its aesthetic is intruded and influenced by market relations. Especially exchange of commodities in the market produces several ruptures in the socially woven relations of communitarian life and introduces an element of commerce and control over means of production. The realm of the domestic disappears from the realm of the market as the market relations command a mode of production that produces with a motive of garnering surpluses from every possible source. In effect by changing the ownership pattern from community to individuals, market relations establish a direct and indirect control over basic factors of production that are hitherto utilized in the realm of the domestic and thereby affects the domestic and brings it out in the field of market forces. How this happens could be understood by noticing a continuous tendency of womenfolk running several local markets and selling domestic and local products. The force of the market change the social relations of gender from partners of production to generators of surplus through the market and it breaches the role assigned to women in terms of their productive labour within the community. While such a bringing of women at the marketplace does not allow a total control over community production and resources by the market forces, it makes a partial possibility of women acquiring market surpluses to use it for their productive role, which is already assigned by the community. The situation marks a response of the communities of the NEI in not leaving vital resources to the market forces, but it shows the use of productive labour in regulating the surplus that comes from the market. Therefore, introduction of market forces at the primary sector of the economy only appears as the dominant pull without being able to change the ground rules of production and exchange, rather it brings in only a different participation of community in regulating the market forces. In other words structural relations of production and reproduction get altered with the intrusion of market forces, while it merely reproduces the social relations within a changed role of actors (Krishna, 2001)

Without having any foundational role within communities of NEI, market forces act through the conduit of State and Private sector that merely helps displacing of resources on which community does not have a control. This produces an immediate concern for the absence of any normative basis for carrying out a practice that weakens the resource base of the place to which the communities belong. Also it is through the relations of production at the primary sectors of the economy that an ontological sense of belonging to the place grows in the community and market relations directly violate that sense of place. So also it enters into an immediate contradictions with the moors of production and operates by way of suppressing the force of resistance that is embedded in the primary relations of production.

This fundamental contradiction between market forces and the primary mode of production perpetuates into contradiction between coexistence of various modes of production and its correlated modes of development producing a diachronic relationship between Culture and Economy, which further results into a politics of resolving irresolvable contradictions in the sphere of production. Obviously it leads to a contest of faculties between various groups and sections representing strata, which is tied to a particular mode of production.

Analytical Framework

Major contributions to elite middle class paradigm come from scholars like Alam (1983), Dhar (2001), Phukan (1983), Bhuyan (1990) and can be summarized in the following:

Investment of Capital Approach

Alam (1983), Dhar (1994), Bhuyan (1990), Sachdeva (1999) propound a theory of increased state investment in primary of economy and secondary sectors and identifying development within the indexes like per capita income, growth of SDP, literacy rate etc. They point out lack of industrial development, deficiency of capital and technical obsolescence as key markers of underdevelopment and extol a path of privatization and private investment in the industrial sector and advocates for a liberal tax regime by the state government. This approach ignores pauperization and proletarianization of the rural pooı, tribal and other marginalized sections of various NEI societies and emphasizes on macro-economic indicators. Further this fails to take into account the social complexities of economic redistribution and local factors that determine levels of productive participations in the economy.

Class, Strata and Role Analysis

In contrast to the above, there are approaches with a more cross-sectional view of development as a historical process where actors like State and classes play the determining role and does not see economy in isolation from politics. It searches out how investment decisions affect various strata of people and how various sectors of economy in turn are affected by the real life conditions of these strata. Noteworthy contributions like Gohain (1973, 1980), Guha (1974,1977), Sharma (1990), Bhattacharjee (1989) conceive development as development investment in public infrastructure and accessibility of resources to various classes. Development is understood in terms of empowerment and disempowerment of various classes by this group of scholars often linking it to strategies of political mobilization, ideological hegemony and control over state power. This group of scholars identifies positions of classes within the nexus of State, polity, and market as actors and players rather than drawing development as an overall effect of economic activities. Their evaluation of underdevelopment consists in disempowerment and marginalization of rural masses, agricultural labourers and tribals. It also consists in political pressure groups organized by the elites formed for larger share of resources and power.

Approach from Politics of Everyday

The primary search in this approach is for social and economic roots of political conflicts. Towards this everyday politics and its ramifications in terms of Development and the roles of various strata are taken as the data and the classical political economy formula 'social reality and the social relations of production determines the consciousness' are taken to be the epistemic determinants of any analysis of socio-economic forces. In a sense the dichotomy between the base and the superstructure is explained away by interpreting base in terms of superstructure. Critically speaking this is a strategy of combining Marxist critique of economism and Gramsci's understanding of culture in terms of everyday politics. Further this approach problematizes political economy explanations of Development in categorical terms like production relations, class relations and surplus value, while it corroborates such categories in terms of the rationality of political mobilization.

It is worthwhile to mention here the debate on Assam Movement as a paradigm for this approach from everyday politics. While Guha

(1977) and Gohain (1980) maintained that Assam Movement is chauvinist in character, Baruah (1989) and Misra (1988) maintained that it's a class struggle against the dominant class formations and an assertion of Assamese middle class nationalism in which broad sections of masses participated against the threat to their livelihoods and habitations. The rationale of Assam Movement directed at the foreign immigrants carried with it underdeveloped productive forces in agriculture as well as relative deprivation of Assam in particular and NEI as a whole in terms of drains of resources and flights of Capital from the periphery to the centre. The usual political economy explanations for marginalization of peasantry has been the bourgeoisie- landlord nexus while they argued that it is land alienation compounded with external control of the local market as experienced by the peasantry is at the root of marginalization. Similarly, middle class assertions are against the dominant national Capital, which hitherto worked against the cultural and political economy of the Assamese people.

Such deviations of understandings revise categories of political economy in terms of everyday politics and articulations of interests. It is noticeable that the validity of political economy explanation is made to supervene upon the validity of political. A core description of linguistic nationalism or demands for political autonomy brought somewhat deeper reality of political economy such as drains of resources from NEI or uneven development between states into common sense reality. In other words what Marx called the 'immanence of political economy' makes transitions from economic to the political and once such as a transition is made it redefines the terms of political economy.

Approaches From Cultural Politics

The major focus of this approach could be summed up as follows-

(a) How cultural identities are shaped thorough fuzzy markers of ethnicity, language and religion and how such markers assume material content in terms of concrete political economy categories. Studies like Verghese (1995), Hazarika (2001) show that cultural identities are product of demand for livelihood and legitimate belonging to a place. Verghese in particular highlights the traditions of belonging to cultures that assume a worldview exclusive to its own locale and non- representation of such a worldview within the parameters of India's democracy. Baruah (1999) emphasizes on the cultural membership and political imageries of belonging to a poly-ethnic State is articulated in the form of sub-nationalism. This focus does not consider political economy as the source of expression of identity rather it abandons economic relations in the distinctions between various classes. It internally focuses on the elites as the leaders of cultural identities while it refuses to look into the roots of elites in economic relations.

(b) Another variety of explanation is through politics of the elites as given by Phukan (2001). This explanation focuses on the conflict of interests between elites already placed within rigidly defined ethnic groups each trying to tilt the political institutional arrangements to their favour and thereby trying to garner prosperity and development. Although this explains one of the major sources of inter-ethnic conflicts and conflicts between pan-Indian identities and regional identities but does not explain why external interventions create a divide or rift between say tribals and non-tribals and also how elites of a particular group attains superiority over others. In a little improved version of this approach comes from Dev (1998,2001) who emphasizes on the lack of normativity in acquisition of political and economic resources within the opportunistic structure of the state. It explains why and how social basis of dominance create asymmetries between competitors. But both these kinds of explanations do not take into account the structural factors for inherent weaknesses of inter elite relationships rather it takes structural factors to be conducive for 'creating the cake' and then focuses on the fight over its share.

(c) Yet another explanation comes from Butola (1996,1997,1998,2002) that accounts how cultural identities are sublimated within the relations of production and how these processes of sublimation express itself in political terms. Butola reinstates interpretation of superstructure in terms of the base in order to show how classes emerge through cultural identities. An extended version of this is also available in Dawar (1996,1997) in terms of roles played by articulation through symbols in marginalized communities by continuously over coming disabilities imposed on them by the dominant political and social order. What these disabilities produce is contestation with dominant symbols and re articulation of the collective identity of the community from positions of weakness.

To sum up, all the above four approaches do not establish a distinct causal relationship between the political economy understanding of level of development and cultural and political expressions of ethnic struggle against the dominance. If dominance is conceptualized in terms of production relations, class relations, modes of production these approaches do not explain why the non-dominant expresses itself with a difference. In the context of NEI one can begin an inquiry by asking a question - what is to be marginalized and express oneself against this marginalization? Is it a question of coming at par with the dominant and the advanced in terms of development or is it falling in line with the process of development at the national level?

In political economy terms what is important is to explain the possibilities of a kind of assertion by the marginalized in the generalized form of alienation that expresses sumtotal of appropriation and sublimation at the levels of economy and cultures. These processes of appropriation and sublimation are experienced at the level of material reality, which signifies the suppression of generalizable cognitive interests as well as extension of an inter- subjective understanding of domination. Development as a category of expression of production on fulfillment of generalizable interests gets imbricated in these processes of appropriation and sublimation. Once again antagonism of class interests, conflicts over resources and capital and difference of symbolic universe of cultural identities enter into a persisting exchange as constituents of the material reality. In other words the totality of interrelationships of class relations, cultural identity and relations of production produce an ensemble of social relations which has to be understood in its totality and not in terms of fragmented aspects of production relations of everyday politics. So the complexity of the process that goes into the formation of cultural identity is irreducible to economic and social roots and as such specific moves and strategies of political expressions of identities assumes a greater symbolic role which is also somewhat different than the material.

With this background one can raise issues of political economy in relation to cultural identities of NEI. Given that the experiences of development presents a situation of being caught between dichotomies of political institution, regions, state, class interests and production relations, a policy to neutralize this uneven field of dichotomies assume a complete transformation which is somewhat distant. The problem for a researcher is how to explain everyday politics of settling claims over development. Therefore it necessitates one to find out a proper explanation for attempts to alter a) structured relations of production, b) structural forces of production, c) everyday forms of complex functioning of the State. Development happens within these structural parameters that appear in the contingent commonsense reality. In other words there is dialectic between the antagonistic social relations that reproduce a certain structure of development and the possibilities of changing that structures.

Within this kind of structural explanation one has to take key memberslike identities, class interests situated within a structure of development in order to provide a systematic explanation for everyday politics of resistance and accommodation that happens in NEI.

Underdevelopment as a Discursive Category

The major demand for most of the political movement could be summarized as demands for recognition and redistribution. Such demands emerge from i) articulation of interests in public sphere and ii) the way political identities of the subjects of social and political discourse perceive a constitutive lack in achievement at satisfactory level of development. Both articulation of interests and the perception of the lack assume status of prime movers in a discourse of demanding redistribution from what Bardhan(1984) called the 'overpowering state'. At another level the limitations of localized forces of production make an absence of dominance of the state while at the same time it makes conspicuous a peripheral collective identity seeking a greater share of resources. In case of NEI the overpowering state is an elitist articulation while the relative absence of the State and the consequent presence of the local communities make collective identities restive for a greater accommodation, but these two layers of mobilization most often converge even without a corresponding convergence between State and local relations of production and thereby showing the potential of elite articulation of interests by inverting the marginalized. Elite articulation of interests makes use of the opposition between the global and the local, structural relations of production and local relations of production in order to produce an oppositional structure in the discourse of political rights. Phases like *Assam Movement* (1977-1985), *Mizo National Movement* (1959-1985), *Naga National Movement* (1949-),

Bodo National Movement (1985-) etc. have all mobilized the local against the national and underdevelopment as a category of backwardness of forces of production against images of developed metropolitan regions in order to focus on a process of exploitation and deprivation from which the local communities have suffered. Such a mobilization by the elite has always been mass based and hence it produced an alliance between classes in a certain locality. This broad based alliance between masses has voiced against a process of development that has led to depletion of local resources and consequent weaknesses of the forces of production.

In a sense, weaknesses of the economy have to sustain it self and to generate viable resources of livelihood results into a situation demanding rapid doses of investment and scarcity of income, employment and other basic resources. The nature of this crisis demonstrates lack of development of productive forces and failure of redistribution. Also this demonstrates an un-appropriated periphery of large agricultural base containing within itself several blockages. The major blockages are: a large labor surplus in rural sector, unutilized natural and mineral resources. In a combination of these blockages a disability of resources is created that further pushes such peripheries as zones of exclusion from any developmental initiatives. Such an exclusion results into an appropriation of local resources by various agencies purchasing produces at a cheaper price. The nexus between such agencies and the local elites reach up to the level of State and other developmental agencies, which acts as the major obstacle in turning the periphery to be self-sustainable. The ironical role of the elites of the progressive sections of society is weakening productive forces, which creates a systematic dependence of the peripheries in the internal structure of exchange relations. Peripheries thereby exist only as a component in the unstinted exchange of resources and products for a song. In other words underdevelopment of the peripheries is not only a product of blockages in the pathways of development of production relations but it is also a product of unstinted one-way exchange from periphery to powerful agencies within the internal structures of the economy.

Given this unequal exchange relationships one has to explain how do the masses of the periphery benefit from participation in political mobilization that bases itself on the dichotomy between the global and the local, the structural relations of production in local relationship. As the political discourse directs the masses against the drain of material and financial resources by agencies like the State and private sectors it merely results into alterations in distribution without strengthening the economic base. This explains why a call for redistributed justice such as greater share of developmental funds and loans for the internal peripheries generate an internal support and explain why benefits do not penetrate to the periphery. In other words the existing unequal relations of exchange, weaknesses of productive forces and structural relations of uneven development perpetuate through such elite driven movements for redistribution. Elites being situated within the community can pit the community against such structural relations of uneven development and can secure rationalizable interests for the community.

In such securing of the community at the peripheries of NEI there is a displacement of production relations i.e. relations between factors of production into a relations between seller and buyer: producers as sellers and merchants as buyers necessarily results into overdose of profit in the chains of reproduction of primary products. At the collective level of the community the rational economic interests of the producers have never been satisfied within such an uneven exchange relation and this keeps the producers at the receiving end. At the collective level these producers are an aggregation of individual interests of the community, which has to be benefited only in a process that removes disadvantages of exchange relations. The displacement of weaknesses of relations of production into a correlative mechanism for an uneven exchange relations contribute to the role of elites in mediating the dichotomies of structural relations of development. Through such mediations the clamor for greater political autonomy and recognition of distinct cultural identities aim at strengthening the collective economic strength in an unequal exchange relationship.

These patterns of mobilization of collective economic interests of the community centers around claims over means of production and ownership of resources. Being regulated by agencies like the State, market and the financial institutions, the claims of the community are tailored to suit the structural relations of production that place communities of NEI at a weaker position of bargaining.

The weaker positions of bargaining is felt at the level of coordination of fundamental properties of economic structure of dominance and social structure of classes which together influences power relations that flow through the overall institutional network as well as incorporation of various cultural groups within the guaranteed sphere of society. The weaker bargaining positions is expressed in a competitive situation of facing the 'others' and such a competition gives a reciprocal confirmation of the experience of positioning and constitute a sense of reality that guides strategies and practices. The immanence of political economy i.e. production relations and exchange relations his in reproducing an asymmetric positioning of a collective layer of production and exchange. The elite subsumption of the underclass in the peripheries, the subsuming of regional elites by the national elites and a dependence of livelihood resources on the inflow and outflow of capital as part of market relations are repercussions of the structural relations of production and reproduction that are manifested in the generalized space of the society.

The antagonistic nature of production relations is expressed through the domain of cultural identities. The way boundaries of communities and cultures are defined it takes into account a typified and specific strength and weaknesses of the bargaining capacity, as it is present in the domain of exchange relations. Cultural identities get consolidated around a position within exchange relationship while it regulates with these positions in conjuncture with a number of correlated, diverse and ethnically different communities. It moves in a space of unequal relationships that marks a mutually contrasting poly-ethnic social space. Organized and unorganized claims of strategic demands and mobilizational formations move in a trajectory of mutual responses. On the one hand, it produces an identity constantly evolving in response to others and on the other hand it tries to consolidate itself in a process of appropriation and reappropriation. Understanding this process of appropriation and reappropriation is not just a strategic exercise apart. It's a process of configuring how such identities are oriented towards an intelligible self-understanding within the limits determined by material conditions.

Modes of elite mobilization at the periphery and the space of inter-community negotiation and competition formed within the structures of relations of production leaves several markers of level of development. In case of NEI a symptomatic description of political mobilization through its contested histories would reveal when, how and why of the discursive construction of underdevelopment. The basic constructions of dichotomy, displacement of production relation into exchange relationships and structuration of cultural identities within a space of context bear specific markers of development/underdevelopment, which would be discussed in details.

The Emergence of NEI as a Socio-political Category

Theoretical Backdrop

Historically speaking the development of NEI was prompted by integration of *Asomiyas* with rest of the country. In economic terms expansion of tea gardens, establishments of centralized British administration were the beginning points of unification of NEI as a group of diverse tribes and nationalities. The share of plurality of communities situated at various stages of socio-economic formations was brought together under the colonial and the postcolonial Indian State. The Major landmarks of this inclusion is described as the positive and negative theses:

TableNo. 6

Positive and Negative Theses of Sequences of Development in NEI

Positive Thesis	Negative Thesis
i) Contact with colonial and early nationalist education, administration, and health care and in general various aspects of modernity (Misra, 2000)	i) Little communities especially tribals were sensitized to defend themselves precisely and process of accumulation started (Prabhakar, 1974).
ii) Spread of individual identity, liberal democratic values and assuring of inter-community social space (Miri, 1996,2003)	ii) Break down of collective identity, communitarian living and emergence of sense of difference with others (Karna, 1990)
iii) Exposure to market forces and commodification of traditional economy (Fernandes, 2001)	iii) Rise of clas difference and aggrandizement for power, money and status (Phukan, 2002)
iv) Participation in electoral politics and democratic governance (Akoijam and Bhagat, 2002)	iv) Sub-national dilution of the customary social institutions and displacement of communities into the vortex of competitive individualism (Nag, 1993)
v) Rise of a collaborating upper caste and upper class swearing by the ideals of the Indian nationalism (Gohain, 1973).	v) Rise of sub-nationalist tendencies and demand of ethnic, cultural and national autonomy (Baruah, 1999)
vi) Commercialization of social relations of production and its benefits percolating through strata (Gohain, ibid.)	vi) Sharp inequalities between various strata and absence of social justice (Dev, 2002)

Although the above characterization is not exhaustive but it provides a sequence of development in terms of effects which could be classified as culturally significant. Looked from a political economy point of view the ensemble of social relations of production is manifested in these sequences of development. Although symptomatically it provides an evaluation of levels of development that certainly draws a picture of ground reality.

What emerges out of these sequences of development and its various symptoms is a political, economic and social process of material reality that could constitute the coordinates of social and political life. The affirmation of cultural identities through a space structured by relations of production formed blocs of political and social structures that define and determine the shape of things to come.

An analysis of the positive theses demonstrates the political and social space of NEI was opened up for interventions by dominant discourse of Indian State and its attendant capitalistic social and economic formations. It provided a ground for an economic and political rationality of hierarchical social order organized along the lines of pre-capitalistic caste, tribes and community formations. The already existing tribal and linguistic communities adjusted themselves to these lines of social formation in mutual and reciprocative arrangements of building up a common national space. Such reordering of an otherwise differentiated and separated social and cultural space through the nationality of Indian State, which for all the purposes intended an unconditional acceptance of the ideology of nationalism. Given this characteristics of reordering within a structure of governance and development assume the form of struggle over the State guided distribution. It also initiated a regime of accumulation hitherto unknown to the traditional social order of NEI and opened up the possibility of furthering economic interests through the play of market forces. What followed from this were a collaborative enterprise and a coalition between the aspirant upper castes of various communities with the harbingers of national Capital striking deeper roots in subsuming the region under the political authority of various institutions of Indian State. Question arises as to what extent this mode of participation brought a reliable base for collective development. The burden of colonial exploitation i.e. the drain of resources and factors of production moving away from the NEI to the mainland of India has irreversible flight of capital. The only difference was heavy doses of public investment with obvious distributional loopholes that merely provided a parallel institutional network for the State and market led development. But the contradictions between the flights of the capital, drain of resources and State sponsored regional development got channelized into emergence of a collaborative middle class, which vacillated between a sense of gain and a sense of losts. This historical trajectory of development soon produced its underside of several fissures within what seemed to be a political and economic integration.

Negative theses are about which process of integration focus on the impact of flight of capital and the State run developmental packages, the flight of capital produced a sense of disempowerment, a sense of being dominated by the Indian Capital which brought about radicalization of primordial of identities. It initiated a process of self-enclosed construction of cultural identity; a reaction against being subordinated and it took that reaction out in extra-constitutional means of politics. The dependence on State run planning and doses of investment led to an accumulating middle class trying to catch up with the trendy market waves. There was a growth of huge consumer class operating within of expandable limits of their income generated through public investment. This replaced the self-reliant nature of belonging to collective identities and developed a parasitic dependence on public investment. Both these component of social and cultural formations marked a radicalization of their identity and their sense of dependence emerged into a number of regional interest groups articulating themselves into the sphere of politics. Such articulations have its ingredient from instances of lack such as failures of governance in health, education and other infrastructural aspects and as such tried, to mobilize economic grievances within articulation of political interests. The language of relationships of reproduction got translated into the language of difference between various strata, linguistic communities and others to evolve a secular language of protests, dissent and résistance.

Further, this language of politics expanded the scope of contestation from the sphere of legitimate public grievances to electoral contest what was essence of backwardness and relative deprivation now occupies the cent stage of radicalization i.e. turning cultural identity into a resistant political identity in its constraints of a communitarian identity. The flight of capital and accumulation was turned into an impediment of growth of productive forces most awkwardly visible in sectors like industry and agriculture.

The emergence of such a political identity spurred a contest of assertion between communities defined with sufficiently distinct features. Anthropological and cultural features were mobilized as symbols in realm of struggle against the dominant perceived as the 'other', the extraneous sources of authority built within the structure of State. This mobilization involved interpretation of the extended meanings of cultural markers in such a way that it gives a sense of authenticity. The emergence of State and market as agencies of development mediated the possibility of inducing political and economic relations into realm of contest between identities by positing structural relations of social dominance. Such a transformation of political economy into emergence of contesting political identity through language of power and cultural symbols turned the material reality into a field of imaginary production of communities. This provided an opportunity for the impoverished and marginalized of the rural sector to express themselves in highly condense, emotional and volatile notions of belonging to a community by placing themselves against an imagined 'other'. Although there is no transformation of the space of economic production, the marginalized from that space becomes an equal subject along with others into articulation against flight of capital and thereby experience a symbolic merger between an urban space and a rural space. This process of transmutation of the consciousness of the commoner and an ordinary member of the community undergoes several layers of transition: from fields of agricultural production to reproduction of these relations of production into a discourse of political resistance. The character of pre-capitalist appropriation of surplus generated out of agriculture is projected into the collective suffering of the community in which elites become the sympathizers of those who suffer by displacing relations of production into exchange relationships. This is also a displacement of native cultural symbols into a contest with dominant cultural symbols that raise a sharp boundary between the self and the other.

Mobilization of Asomiya *Identity*

'Asomiya' identity as a paradigm case of transformation of political economy into a radical cultural identity would demonstrate the actual process of how political economy implies cultural resistance. A skewed relation of production resulting into an extraneous control of means of production has been the issue in formulating a singular notion of *Asomiya* identity. The industrial sector constituted by over 960 odd tea gardens mostly owned by the pan-Indian companies, over 40 percent of the agricultural land being occupied by the non-*Asomiya* population and consequent land alienation was compounded by the gradual decline of the number of Assamese speakers in terms of percentage of population between 1911 to 1971 (Baruah, 2000) and consequent increase of the names of immigrants in the voters list produced a sense of lost among the *Asomiya* as a community. The apprehension of a rapid demographic change due to immigration from Bangladesh, other neighboring countries as well as immigration from other states of Indian mainland sparked off a huge protest against the totality of the scenario of domination by non-Asomiya communities. Question arose how safe is the *Asomiya* community from being losing its distinct identity? The Assam Movement spearheaded by the All Assam Students Union (AASU) involved the rural peasantries and the middle classes who were directly responding to the process of marginalization manifested in key areas of social life in a sense that the State sponsored and market driven forces could not generate development for which it didn't have any answer. This unwarranted consequence produced an image of the Indian State similar to the colonial British administration engaged in plundering and exploiting Assam. This had resulted into a thesis about internal colonization of Assam and the NEI is like a colonial hinterland being drained by agencies of development. Such a concern that supports the notion of *Asomiya* identity with the question of autonomy in the sphere of larger question about share of resources like land, forest, output from industry being taken away visible non-indigenous set of actors produced a sense of crisis engulfing the totality of being an *Asomiya*. Assam Movement reacted violently against such a crisis only to come to the position that various sections of people affiliated themselves to the *Asomiya* identity can save the impending danger. In other words crisis at the level of economy could generate an identity crisis, which was displaced into crisis of defining who is an *Asomiya* of various strata and classes within the relations of production. It has not been possible to arrive at synthetic notion of *Asomiya* identity. Rather it incorporated all those who identified themselves as Asomiya irrespective of whether they belong to the language and culture. This amounted to the deconstruction of identity of those who recently had got incorporated voluntarily within the ambit of *Asomiya* identity. They had been identified as neo-Assamese mostly belonging to the peasantries of lower Assam and also became citizen by naturalization as recently as 1950s. It further showed the cleavage between the agrarian relations of production and capitalistic modes of production in industries without a convergence i.e. not being able to resolve contradictions between the nature of accumulation in those kinds of relations. While the agrarian relations led to formation of *Asomiya*, the nature of appropriation in the non-indigenously owned sectors of production produce an appropriation of cultural and linguistic identities as well.

The Bodo *Movement*

Bodos are a distinct group of plain tribals, which had defined themselves as a tribe within *Asomiya* identity (Choudhury, 1996). This sense of being a part of *Asomiya* identity was dependent on the level of recognition from upper cast elites within *Asomiya* nationality (Dev, 2001). But such a condition of inclusion turns into an experience of exclusion by the Assamese elites when there is a visible difference of treatment in concrete socioeconomic and cultural terms. Rather the terms of recognition are not mutually reciprocative, it was set by the necessities of political assertion of *Asomiya* as an identity, within which an inclusion of tribal social relations was necessary. But such an inclusion was carried out only to the extent that tribal social relations do not generate a breach with relations of middle class and elite domination. As *Bodos* were weak in terms of middle class and educated elites at a cultural level, so the tribal social relations only could find a place of subsumption within the larger economic relations between *Bodos* and Assamese (Narzary 1998). What hitherto remained as a subterranean feature of *Asomiya* in the form of subsumption of tribal social relation within the middle class formation of Assamese identity suddenly assumed a different significance when *Bodos* were not allowed to be represented in the final outcome of Assam Movement, ending with what is called the Assam Accord signed between upper caste and elite leaders of All Assam Students' Union and Govt. of India. Such a political exclusion bore its effect in the self-conscious clamour of *Bodos* for a separate *Bodo* language and Bodo culture unaccomodatable within the fabric of Asomiya identity. It once again reflected the disjunctions between the peripheral tribal modes of production and elite modes of development within *Asomiya* middle classes (Misra, 1998). The *Bodos* organized themselves against the discrimination through governmental apparatus controlled by the *Asomiya* elite. The tribal characterization of Bodos bearing incommensurable relations with nationality aspirations of Asomiya identity also reflects a contradiction between the *Bodo* identity and *Asomiya* as a pan-Indian formation.

Economic Practices as Sources of Cultural Difference

Apart from such distinctive approach at the plane of culture, difference in livelihood and economic practices create boundaries that act as markers of variation in development. Let us take two examples – the *Apatani* of Arunachal Pradesh and *Angami* Naga of the state of Nagaland.

The *Apatanis* of Arunachal Pradesh go by certain signs of reality to decide about whether they should go for hunting or cultivation. The signs for inauspicious cultivation are-

- When bride and groom are childless after many years of marriage
- When domesticated fowls and animals are handicapped
- When bees or snakes or other strange insects enter the house or granaries and when a man dreams of a banana tree or mushroom growing at the house etc.

Although such signs are a part of their belief structures, which is culturally construed, the economic activities are determined by such physiographic-psychological considerations. If the signs are not favourable then they will rear *mithun* and oxes. Apparently indicators of good or bad omen and signifiers of intuitions of what is going to come through the activity of production, these actually are considerations about various factors of production, their availability and levels of use. An accounting of reproductive labour (necessary for assessing the present and future generation of cultivators and their state of health and a host of gender specific responsibilities), levels of storage of domesticated animals and an assessment of animal health (necessary for environmental, utilitarian and food security purposes), assessment of availability of flora and fauna that require fruition by various insects and an assessment of activity level in the hearth and the animal hygiene- all constitute the worldview of cultivation bearing specific marks of rationality which is very different from the 'modern', yet so self-sustaining. The anthropological markers within the factors of production and the sense of practising cultivation through those markers make the character of their mode of production culturally and anthropologically very different from some such culture with a similar mode pf production.

But the sheer specificity of resource use by a tribal community in NEI can't be generalized except by way of empirically showing how it is done. In the following (a table mapping use of non-timber resources is appended:)

Table No. 7

Some of the Non-timber Forest Produce Used by Arunachali Tribes

Bamboo	
Dendrocalamus hamiltonii	Kako
Bambusa tulda	Jathi
Bambusa balcooa	Boluka
Bambusa pallida	Bijlii
Bambusa nutans	Mokai
Dendrocalamus gigantaus	Sadiya kako
Phllostatchys pubescence and many other species	
Cane	
Calamus stenuis	Jati
Calamus floribundus	Lejai
Calamus flagellum	Raidang
Calamus latifolius and five other species	Houka
Plant leaves, fruits etc.	
Thysanolaena maxima	Broom grass
Imparta cylindrica	Thatch grass
Illicium griffthii	Lichi
Livistona jackinsiana	Toko leaves
Calamus erectus	Jang leaves
Pinus roxburghii	Resin
Canarium strictum	Dhuna
Piper peclcpuloides	Pipli
Persea species	Jigat bark
Taxus baccata	Leaves
Coptis teeta	Medicine

Source: Shukla, GP& K.Haridasan(1996)

In a similar way the sheer contingency of production of horticultural items would show that the anthropological belief that is discussed above is a reflection of the reality of horticultural and fruit production. In the table below one could see the diversity of fruit production that would explain the contingency of those beliefs. Further production of fruits as a horticultural item opens up the possibility of unexplored potential of marketing, but so far there is no substantive investment in processing and preservation of these products. It could be easily understood that marketing such products of domestic modes of production would have strengthened the economic base of *Arunachali* communities which does not fit with the goal of maximizing returns to industry or returns in the form of payoff from infrastructural investments. Discrimination against culturally produced items and its supportive infrastructure operate as a major rationale for under privileged production of such indigenous goods. This also shows the skewed emphasis on infrastructure and services that do not have any roots in the local mores of the communities (Choudhury, 1998). The table below would show the culturally preferred horticultural items that are in extensive use in Arunachal Pradesh.

Table No. 8
Some Horticultural Products by Arunachali Tribes

Fruits
Duchesnea indica (yellow strawberry)
Morus spp. (mulberry)
Myrica esculenta (bay berry/ box myrtle)
Prunus acuminata, P.cornuta, P. jenkinsiii, P. nepaulensis (all plums)
Pyrus pashia (pear)
Ribes gracialle (a currant)
Rubus lineatus (a red berry), *R. ellipticus* (yellow rasberry), *R. lasiocarpus, R. moluccanus* (black cherry), *R.reticulates.*

Vegetables
Abellmoschus maniho (a hibiscus)
Cucumis trigonus (a cucumber)
Luffa graveolens (a gourd)
Neoluffa sikkimensis

Source: Shukla, GP& K.Haridasan (1996).

In contrast to such anthropological structuring of economic productions, *Angamis* in the state of Nagaland choose their field for cultivation only if the following physiographic conditions are fulfilled:

> Sounds generated by blowing of buffalo horns, which echo from one of the hills and if the echo echoes at least three times from the surrounding hills and if there is slippery slope showing the possibility of flow of water on other side of the hill means that there won't be flood on this side of the hill meant for cultivation.

– There would be enough water on the reservoir on the other side of the hill

The above three conditions show that an indigenous process of knowing whether a field is enough productive or a discerning through the trial and error method by taking into account the right kinds of echoes. Although *Angamis* follow domestic mode of production it is the culturally significant difference in practices of productions that goes into a production of distinctive identities. Therefore the anthropological roots of cultural practices occupy a significant place is defining the tribal identity. Development understood in terms of such indigenous cultural practices unsettle the dichotomy of development and underdevelopment generated by extraneous factors of State and market. Looked from an anthropological point of view State and market can act as an antithesis of the historically enclosed self-defined processes of development. The balance of livelihood practices and the use of resources within an economy based on culture invalidates the need for external sources of investment and follows a path of endogenous processing of inputs. This path of development from within not only resists those relations of production that reproduces the internal relations of production at the level of generalized commodity production, but it also sustains the maximum potential of production by avoiding sources of contradiction within the forces and factors that are constitutive of the indigenous economy.

The crux question in understanding social and cultural processes in NEI is, *do the communities move up on the trajectory of development to emerge into secure and stable identities that could catch up their relative backwardness from the better-off counterpart?* Moving up through the structure of relations of production scaled in the Colonial policy of exclusion and Post-Colonial politics of regional discrimination (Misra.T, 1980), the NE-Indian communities, today, are recoiled onto themselves and poised to offer challenges to the homogenizing and hegemonizing processes of development. The primary response to any major industrial project is a social awareness of the potential depletion of resources endemic to it and anything is welcome if the possibility that the 'sense of place' for people from within rather than without is guaranteed. It is in this responsive milieu of NEI that many of the major industrial and developmental projects carry out not only the assigned task of productivity and growth, but also remains accountable to political and social vigil from NE-Indian communities. The question is, given the delicate and exceptional social fabric of NE-India communities, how do the Indian State and other developmental agencies respond to the critical vigil on them in various sectors of economy?

In the wake of a globalized national economy, the state of Economy of the NEI does not provide a ready infrastructural base for heavy investment, nor does the communities open up to the hues of cultural globalization. Rather NE-India gives stiff challenge to any attempt of appropriation of cultural and ethnic identities by the sweep of market forces, yet it still enjoys a 'sustainable lifestyle' in both material and non-material terms. Such a 'sustainable lifestyle' already embedded in the culture/communities of NEI is rather an exception to the otherwise poverty stricken and socially impoverished backyards of national mainstream. Neither the welfarist nor the entrepreneurial frameworks of development can ground itself here beyond offering 'palliatives'. In other words, the life-world moorings of NE-Indian communities are still to be affected by system-bound, agency-bound or State-bound policies of development in a fundamental way. Rather, the process of development of an identity, socially and culturally grounded within communities of NEI has confronted the ill effects of developmental projects that contributed to social differentiation and mainstreaming of distinct cultural identities.

From an advocacy point of view, NEI presents a fit case for descriptions like back-ward, undeveloped and weak that prompt the need for free flow of factors of production, especially foreign investment and capital goods. The advocacy takes the form of 'policy' prescriptions like opening trade routes with neighbouring countries, especially with South West China, Bangladesh and Myanmar. It also prescribes further infrastructural developments like improving communication through land, river and air routes and a better governmental support system to investors from outside. One can stumble upon a number of other such stylized prescriptions emanating from neo-classical concerns for developing markets in backward regions, but the crucial question is, *did NEI not develop because of an absence of such policy prescriptions or is it because of certain other structural constraints?* To put the record straight, one should ask, what really contributed to 'Peripherilization' of NE-Indian economy? One way to answer the question is to locate a process of alienation of the NEI within the very developmental policies that have been followed by the Indian State. Obviously, the other way is to put the blame on certain unfriendly factors that grew within NE-India. The first way would reveal more about the core mechanism of developmental process.

Regimes of Underdevelopment in NEI: The Local and the Global

How the agencies of developments perpetuate a regime of underdevelopment could be understood from the fact that one of the important mineral resource, oil, produced in oilfields of Assam provides the glaring example of a simultaneous plundering of resources as well as depletion of capacity of the State in question. Oil production in Assam grew from 0.1 m tonnes in 1962 to 5 million tonnes per annum by 1970's. It is projected that by 2019 the crude oil production shall reach its exhaustible limit. But what is most agonizing is the discriminatory rates of share of revenues between Central and State government. During mid-eighties the royalty paid to Assam went from Rs.325 per tonne to its current rate at Rs.632 per tonne, while the Central government earns on an average a dividend of Rs.2623/- per tonne. What is even more disturbing is the fact that two third of Assam's oil is taken out to feed various refineries outside Assam. When Assam demanded a refinery with an optimum capacity to refine the crude produced in oilfields of Assam, it got only a toy refinery, currently being installed at Numaligarh. Like this draining of oil resources, there is a drain of profit from tea industries of Assam. The magnitude of the drain could be understood in these figures: during the period 1962-1999, Assam was producing an average 250 million kg tea per year. Given the international price of tea at $2.5 per kg, the total sale value would have come to some 5,250 million dollars. Of this huge amount, tea companies, needless to say, have invested almost nothing back in Assam.

These example do not only evince that resources from NEI are drained out and turned into sources of profit in national and international markets, but what it further points to is the unleashing of a chain of exploitative network that shifts the outputs of development from NE-Indian region. Further it turns the mineral, forest and other natural resources of the region into an attractive storehouse and thus inviting hawks from outside to operate through various developmental institutions. Another stark example is the plundering of forests from NEI to national and international markets. The depletion of forests is so fast that it is shown in a National Remote Sensing Agency projection that in Assam while forests covered 33% land area during 1985-86, it has gone down drastically to 24% in 1995-96. This projection of a possible depletion of forests in other NE-State as well produced a knee-jerk reaction from various quarters, including the supreme court of India disbanding all kinds of logging in any part of NEI. The result of such knee-jerk reaction was that forest-based industries and supply of wood is affected so badly that the livelihood of a large number of mill owners and wage earners is at stake. The failure of the Supreme Court to take into account the indigenous methods of replenishment and growing of forests in a traditional forest-based economy like Meghalaya or Arunachal Pradesh dealt a heavy blow on the economy of the region. Rather the blanket ban on rise of forest for the purpose of domestic and market needs has encouraged only poachers and mafias, who in collusion with State machinery continue rampant exploitation of forest resources and it's trafficking within and outside the national borders. Further, the Supreme Court judgment disempowered the forest-dwelling communities and empowered the state to exercise an absolute monopoly of control over forest resources, thereby overthrowing the forest based livelihood and economy completely out of grove in the region. This apparent ban on the local community paradoxically strengthens the institutions and agencies of drain, as it is they who would get a free hand in the market of natural resources, as a large section of local entrepreneurs would be thrown out of market by this act of banning by Supreme Court. This could be understood by observing that markets for other natural resources would exist only, rather the absence of local entrepreneurs dealing with forest resources would result into a depression of their income and thereby generate a greater external thrust to take out permissible resources outside the region. Given this, one would not be wrong to prognosticate that developmental agencies legitimated by the State, be it public sector or be it private sector shall rule over the local producers, as such producers would be paradoxically disbanded for the ostensible reason of depletion of natural resources, while drainage of such resources by there legitimated agencies would go unabated.

Within this process of drain, one can also observe a reverse process of stability in traditional sectors of economy, which are more oriented to participation of the folk. One can call it 'folk economy' that remains untouched from this process of drain. When industrial sectors of the economy do not show much growth except in terms of productivity, which simply means drain of a greater quantity of resources, rise of productivity in agriculture, horticulture or fishing means a greater generation and concentration of income in a larger section of population. Due to such generation of income in period of decline of growth in sectors other than agriculture in Assam during 1997-'02, Regional Rural Banks (RRB) recorded a rise in deposits and credits against quantities during the previous years, which commensurate with higher growth of agriculture and higher generation of surplus income among small farmers and fishermen.

This situation leads us to ask a counter-question to the moorings of globalization. If the moorings of globalization is constituted by a preferential opening up of higher profit yielding sections to external investment agencies and reduction of investment in primary sectors, why does growth in profitable sectors not result in a greater overall growth in economy? Answer to this question is twofold: on the one hand ongoing processes of resource depletion compounded by flight of profit result into registering a low growth rate as such a process can only show high factor cost. On the other, low investment in traditional sectors of economy does not yield high dividends. Therefore caught in this dual process of externalization of more profitable resources, and internalization of less profitable resources, the stereotypical agenda of globalization cannot but result into a general slowdown of economic growth in a region like NE-India marked by its abundant natural resources. But globalization can merely 'naturalize' this dual and mutually opposite processes of externalization and internalization.

Now the archetypal prescriptions for development of NE-India as a 'region' by opening up to neighboring countries and facilitate free flow of factors sound quite post-modern. It sounds 'post-modern' because the prescription affirms cruising the borders and interacting with trade spaces from neighboring countries. But such an idea sounds more like opening up NE-India as part of route from South-western China to Bangladesh and Myanmar. The idea gathers its momentum from its striking assumption that once NE-India becomes a part of the east Asian growth by extending trade route through itself, the impossible barriers erected and maintained between NE-India and India is also bound to totter. The question here is how this idea of trading as a free market activity would reconcile the processes of drain of resources from NE-India (then possibly further drained towards this whole of trading route), which has become the mainstay of its economy?

Leaving this question as an open question, one can look back at how NE-Indian communities move up on this trajectory of internal colonization. Corresponding to the process of externalization of profitable resources there is an externalization of communities and their identities in terms of a national identity that jibes with the national identity construed by Indian State. But such an externalization remains 'unsublimated' just as externalization of resources does not bring back any dividend to the source. Contrarily, the way internalization of resources in domestic sectors of the economy take place keep the community going, in the same way it leads to stabilization and sublimation of the identity with respect to place and culture.

Within this close parallel between globalization and localization of economy and community one can characterize the nature of center periphery relationship between mainstream India and its northeast. As far as externalization is concerned, it is linking up of NE-India with the national market and hence the claims of nation hood for the identity of the community hinges upon this becoming a part of a mainstream. As far as internalization within economy is concerned, it is closely related to the practices of life-world suitability among NE-Indian communities and hence specific to their lived context without any reference to the 'mainstream'. But as mainstream absorbs away vital resources, so, even while NE-India remains attached to the ration-state, yet it can't discover a pan-Indian identity. It at best holds its citizen identity within the Indian mainframe, while it retains its national, cultural and ethnic identity outside this frame.

One can understand the structural constraint in this process of nationalization of social identities of NE-India in a number of ways. Firstly, externalization of the economy produces a reverse pull of retention of cultural identity in its 'local' form and such 'local' forms are treated as constituents of a national identity. Secondly, externalization does not allow local communities to grow as it reduces the drain of the local to a minimum in matters of production and distribution. Thirdly, internalization leads to construction of an identity enclosed to itself or at best extended up to intercultural spaces that are available locally, while such cultural spaces are also restrained due to pulls of 'local' grounding. In other words, neither the external and larger nation space is formed in integration with the local nor the internal or intercultural spaces are formed in conjunction between communities. What emerges from this scenario is a picture of constrained growth of local identities, pulled apart internally and externally to be a part of the larger nation space or intercultural spaces, while such pulls produce its inevitable tension in retention of one's own cultural and ethnic identity.

National and Global Aspects of Development NEI: A Cultural Perspective

There are two broad ways in which discourses of development have dealt with the cultural specificity of the communities of NE-India. One way is by establishing an equivalence or homology between culture and economy in terms of belonging to a common National market, the other by narrowing economy down to cultural settings and yet turning culture itself into a force of development and growth. What is obvious in both these approaches is the attempt to come to terms with specific ethnic cultures which in a large sense remained nonconforming with the modern projects of national development and so it becomes an immediate necessity to make national development conform to specific ethnic cultures. It's were different question whether this idea of coming to terms remain elusive for both the national development and specific ethnic cultures only to generate some kind of a disjunction between them, as analyzed in the previous section. What is significant here now is to track down the kind of development discourse that attempts to negotiate the disjunction.

A typical instance of development discourse could be the kind of commissioned studies made at the behest of government and financial agencies on NEI. Let's take a few cases here for discussion; e.g., Nagaland, Mizoram and Meghalaya. A study (1997) entitled,"Industrial Resource Survey of Nagaland" conducted by Govt. of Nagaland and National Development Research Corporation, New Delhi States,

> *Due to the agrarian nature of the states economy potential for developing agro-based industries should be exploited on priority basis. In terms of natural resources, forest and mineral based industries would deserve similar priority. It would, therefore be necessary to set up industries based on raw materials from outside the state to cater to demand for particular products both inside Nagaland and other market.* (22).

Although the study highlights the general potential of agricultural mineral and forest based industries, but it prescribes something contradictory, that of setting up industries by obtaining raw materials from outside the State. What it implies is an apparent conservation of Nagaland's resources; while it advocate a path which would undesirably make entry of factors of production from outside and thereby raising the cost of production. Seemingly, the dilemma between conserving the resources of the State and developing industries find such otiose expressions in government sponsored commissioned studies. The failure of the study to address the question of what the manifesto of *National Socialist Council of Nagaland* describes as "Nagaland and The Influx of Indian Capital and Indian Nationals" and states,

> *The pouring in of Indian capital in our country, for political resources has shattered the Naga people into a society of wild money. Its accumulation in the hands of the reactionary traitors and the rich has accelerated the process of exploitation and suppression of the people. The appropriation of the vast means of production, distribution and exchange and other means of profit marking by this exploiting class and by the Indian parasites has drawn a distinct line between them and the people.* (62-3)

The answer to this description is couched in the study in terms of setting up of labour-intensive and low capital-intensive industries particularly as the state is facing the problem of growing unemployment. But such terms are merely a cursor to the unmeant and unadjusted disjunction between tribal culture and development. This becomes clear when the study talks of economic significance of cultural specificity of Nagaland in these words,

> *Nagaland offers a varied experience to tourist- picturesque landscapes, vibrantly colourful people with rich tribal tradition in songs, dances, festivals and handicrafts pleasant climate throughout the year, etc. combine together to give a refreshing change in all visitors. Some of the saleable ideas are anthropological tours, trekking, mountaineering, special interest tours, to see tribal life, wild life, scenic beauty or wonders, craftsman centers, museums, botanical gardens, zoos etc.* (72)

Such a spectacular representation of Naga culture from a tourist point of view clearly demonstrate the national developmental agenda from the tribal way of life, despite an undertone of perpetuation of this way of life, the study invokes an anthropological imagery to convert development into an agenda of preserving an ethnic sanctuary in Nagaland without really underlining what kind of cultural ethos has gone into making life so spectacular. The wider undressed issue here is an incompatibility between what is deemed to be an economic utilization of resources from Naga culture and the ethos of Naga life. Such a repertoire remains self-explanatory to explain a supposed inconvertibility of tribal ways of life into a developmental exercise. The report states under a little 'Food Based Industry',

> *Meghalaya has a high percentage of meat consuming population and the climate is congenial for animal husbandry like rearing of cattle, pigs, goats and poultry. In fact, in a survey conducted by N.E.C it is estimated that the meat products consumed in the NEI region are alone worthRs.1000 crores per annum.*

This recognition of specific meat-eating habits of NE-Indian people perhaps arises as a cultural deviancy for the largely vegetarian, non-meat consuming people of the mainstream and works as a hidden source of disadvantage as such a high level consumption is not backed up by a proper planning and development of necessary resources.

One should, therefore, surmise that the mainstay of Statist developmental agenda takes into account the indigenous resources and life styles for a purportedly different purpose of industrialization one which does not jibe with locally managed and developed industries of tribes of NEI.

On the other end of this disjunction between culture and development, there is an ethnographic fiction of grounding a process of sustainable development in the lives of people of the region. A comprehensive study entitled, "A Review of the Social Basis for Sustainable Development in Arunachal Pradesh" done by Elizabeth M. Taylor and circulated by an International Environmental and Development group called 'Future generations' arrive at an exotic and culture specific notions of development. In a poignant analysis it states,

> *Specific features of the landscape become profoundly charged with ultimate cosmological meanings as well as basic social identity and collective history. Whether or not people would be able to articulate abstract notion of ecological homeostasis, the idea of self-correcting and holistic exchanges of energy to balance national and human order is central to this cultural logic.*

Such an understanding of 'cultural' logic smacks of Eurocentric notions of holism as the local and indigenous idea of human intervention in their own landscape follows rather complex 'exchange relations' which are not readily visible, but are rather functionally shaped and embedded in the larger network of social relations. Ignoring such networks of social relations, perhaps, reproduces a fictive ethnography of development germane to the needs of conserving local resources as 'reserves' to be later transformed to products in the global market. We can rather focus upon a symbolic story of cultural development mentioned by Verrier Elwin (1977) in 'Myths of North East Frontier of India'. Elwin puts the story as somewhat common to various tribes of Arunachal Pradesh. The story concerns 'knowledge' of writing or rather knowing in general. It is stated thus,

> *All wisdom was long ago written on pieces of skin and given both to the hill people and people of the plains. But the hungry tribesman cooked and ate their piece of skin, with the result that they have always been ignorant.*

Nobody could say how the binary between knowledge and ignorance entered into tribes to develop a poorer self-image of them, but it speaks of a cultural difference that is nonnegotiable. The difference here is marked by symbolic retention and consumption of the 'skin', obviously involving two different modes of life and an exchange relationship between hill and plain people. It is in this sense, even in the case of knowing the ecology and development relationship and cultural difference with others come into play to give rise to a valuation structure, which can never remain only centered upon endogenous factors, but in some way or the other must make a cut with something exogenous: Therefore, development as a wholly endogenous process as conceived by ethnographic conceptualization of forms of life need to combine a component of comparative assessment of cultural difference without necessarily imbibing the value structure of others.

This kind of a comparative assessment of oneself without imbibing value structures of others is largely reflected in the actual life style of NE-Indian communities. It is worth while to note here that changes in the occupational structure wrought by developmental agenda did not at all affect tribal occupations rather changes in occupational structure left the tribals largely away. Tribals continue their traditional modes of livelihood such as hunting, food-gathering, woodcutting; craftsmanship etc. while one could come to terms with the new the effects of such development as it bypasses its own subjects.

Also the presumed anonymity of living together within a nation and in the context of India, the inheritance of a colonial State mobilizing those specific identities to the anonymity of nation-state is a process of erosion of those specifics. 'Nations from below' spring out from what has been erased in order to counter the signification generated within the State. The immobilized signifiers of identity with which the consciousness of a community identify itself at the bottom of a hierarchy are pulled out with force and that is how within the limits posed by the State, the conditions of making of an identity are effectively altered. The alteration of those conditions such as recovery of one's older faith, rejection of policies of misrecognition operating from the bottom change the field of political discourses radically. Such changes in definitions and privileged interpretations given to an identity extend the space for its self-definition and it appears through a rupture or a disjunction in time and space. The biography of a nation concealing the gaps between law-like succession of history and underdetermined ethnography of peoples slips out in the rupture at the bottom to open up the possibilities of its negation and resistance. Such a ruptured biography of a nation open up different styles of national imagination; it debunks a linearly coordinated narrative of unified nation and bases itself upon the sovereignty of available immediate markers of identity.

5

Conclusion: Phases, Facts and Faces of North-East India

The current chapter aims at summarizing and reflecting upon the paradigms of development that emerges out of our study of "Political Economy of Underdevelopment of North East India and its Cultural Implications". The major paradigm that emerges out of the study is the paradigm of Centre-Periphery relations that shapes the political and cultural spaces of NEI in terms of a process of 'peripherialization' that acts as the leitmotif of production of social identities (Ch.2). The other paradigm that emerges out of the study is that relations of production produces the space in a manner that modes of production determines and gets determined by modes of development and space of production and reproduction sustains a set of structural relations that constitute the multiplicity of modes of production organized in a hierarchy of dominance (Ch.3). Next, such structural relations of production transform modes of production into forces of culturally and socially produced relations of identity that manifest itself in the form of cultural economy. It is observed that cultural economy is an outcome of political economy and in this sense underdevelopment gets grounded in forms of life within which communities wage struggles for survival (Ch.4). All these findings assume the form of a paradigm as these are bound by definite and certain relations of Political Economy, which further assume a characteristic form, that of metropolis-satellite relationship between core of the Indian economy and it's North-eastern periphery. These relations of Political Economy are either processes of accumulation or exchange relations that reproduce the structural relations of Production, which in turn go into sustaining and continuing a given mode of production vis-à-vis a mode of development. The major question that crops up through such paradigmatic relations of production and development is that *how do modes of development sustain and alter the modes of production?* If the relationship between modes of production and modes of development is a deterministic one, doesn't this very relationship resist a mutual affectation of the latter by the former and vice-versa? In other words changes in one are resisted by the other as long as there is a reestablishment of strict and necessary correspondence between the two in their impulse to change. Therefore resistance is endemic in this law like correspondence between modes of production and modes of development. But this endemic nature of resistance is manifested in sustainable relations of production that constitute the cultural economy (ies) of the region that emerges as the other of Capitalist Development. One can go unto surmising that the resistance to capitalist mainstream development is manifested in manifold local economies that establish new equations of exchange beyond the laws of surplus extraction within Global and National development. Such local economies qua cultural economies exist as the weak other of the dominant modes of production in such a manner that whatever reordering of space(s) is done through surplus extraction and development (of underdevelopment) it weaves spaces that are expropriated in this unidirectional flow of surplus from periphery to the centre. Such spaces in the periphery are left as periphery outside the centre, while such peripheral spaces introduce new relations of exchange between social groups and hegemonic forces of capitalism. These spaces exist outside appropriation or rather they are left after appropriation. Geographically such spaces are traditional spaces of cultural economy that acts autonomously of maelstrom of Capitalist world economy, hitherto only understood as pre-capitalist modes of production. But resistances that are endemic between modes of production and modes of development within mainstream turn to these spaces as unreconciled exterior of surplus extracting economy and hence transform these peripheries into autonomous spaces of resistance to the mainstream. Looked from another side such peripheries are needed to be maintained by Capitalism's core in order to sustain the process of extraction and thereby it has to allow a greater autonomy to these left out spaces. The question is, do such peripheries of Capitalism constitute the space of extraction as an excluded essence that emerges in the dialectic between Centre and Periphery, but never merges into the Centre for the fundamental dichotomous relationship that the Centre forebears with the periphery. Such a dichotomous mode of surplus extraction generates its own resistance by a dichotomy between surplus and subsistence that organizes the space of resistance as a space of production and exchange. But how the unequal relationship of exchange is organized in space is a question that brings out the nature of the production of space through unequal exchange, which is the inevitability of an exterior in the form of an irreconcilable periphery as the residue of Capitalist accumulation that stands on the other end of the space of surplus. This dialectic between surplus and its residue operates in the space of production and extends itself to the exterior and the interior by way of separating the periphery from the centre. One could recognize that the logic of capital divides and subdivides the space produced out of extraction of surplus, disjointed from each other in the form of an unmitigable dichotomy of spaces, between whom there is an exchange of unequal kind resulting into appropriation and expropriation at two ends of the spectrum. The laws of Capitalist appropriation have to constantly fill up the gap created by separation of spaces as a function of appropriation and hence develop a synthesis of appropriation and expropriation in a common space. Could the residual space become such a synthetic connector between space of surplus and space of residues?

Posing of these questions partially bring out the complex nature of organization of the space of production and development within Capitalism and spaces are produced in order to sustain the logic of Capital. In the context of the unequal exchange between North-east India and core of Indian economy, the processes of creation of the space of surplus in the centre, separation of centre from the periphery and residual role of periphery etc. assume the form of 'resistance' at each of these moments of Capitalist appropriation. As we have seen from a paradigmatic understanding of the relationship between the modes of production and the modes of development, the determination of the one by the other simultaneously facilitates the production of functional spaces as well as knits them with logic of mutual resistance. Every moment of extraction of surplus is met with a counter moment of holding back what is extracted and such a dialectical process initiates an autonomous concatenation of residual spaces through a commonality of functions such as supply of raw and primary resources. The space of resources assumes a distinct natural and cultural form that tries to sustain ecology and a habitat, which are pulled into the process of extraction. Such natural forms and its attendant cultural habitats act as an other of Capital constituting a space prior to the spaces produced by capitalist modes of production. Such a pre-constituted space of non-capital refuses to be a part of capitalist modes of production and thereby produces a problematique of merging such spaces within the space of production as well as within the space reproduced. Such spaces of non-capital also pose the problem of interiorizing capital as it asks the capital to sheer off its logic of appropriation and refuse to yield to the extended reproduction of capital. This relationship between the capital and the other of capital is spatially organized by logic of inclusion in which capital yields to the pre-constituted space of resources by suspending the moment of reproduction. The space of NEI, being a pre-constituted resource space is accommodated within the operation of mainstream Indian capital by a suspension of an extended reproduction of capital over the space of NEI.

Given this incorporation of the space of NEI within the logic of Capital and the resistance to reproduction of Capital, the only way Capital can work is by organizing spaces of production in the form of recycling already available in the self-sustaining little economies of NEI. The domestic mode of production exists in this recycling mode. But Capital disrupts this process of recycling within the domestic mode of production by way of incorporating the domestic within non-reproducible mode of extraction of resources, which weakens the local economies and ensures the flight of resources without an extended reproduction of those resources. Such non-reproduction of resources gets absorbed into a perpetuation of Capital through mere extraction of resources for finished products, a perpetuation of Capital since colonial times. The moment of extraction generates an immediate disjunction between resource base and what is extracted out of it such that extraction produces surplus at the one end and leaves its residues on the other end. Such ends of extraction bifurcates the space of production into a space of supply and a space of flight restraining the productive potential of these resources and thereby blocking an extended reproduction of Capital. Therefore, this character of non-reproducible extraction of surplus heavily falls back on its own residues, which act as a hindrance to the process of extraction. This is the reason why the resource potential is unutilized and unutilized resources are left in a space of residue, while utilized resources exhaust it in producing one-time-surplus. Such a surplus bends itself backward to the resource pool, which is unincorporated without an extension of Capital. As a consequence of one-time-surplus the separation between the space of extraction and the space of resources assume the form of a temporal disjunction that cannot be filled up by organizing the space of reproduction. So, the problem is further compounded as NEI as a periphery gets disjointed from the mechanism of extraction as extraction into the mainland leaves the periphery in itself and as the resource base of NEI does not allow reinvestment of the surplus, reproduction of Capital is possible only if the surplus extraction is carried through stronger linkages with the local sources. In other words, the nature of surplus extraction within the logic of Indian Capital separates NEI as a non-reproducible space of Capital and thereby generating two contradictory processes: one there is flight of resources and the other there is no reproduction of either the Capital or of the resources. This shows a dependency relationship in which NEI looks for an extended reproduction of this resource base while the logic of operation of Indian Capital only gives rise to one-time-surplus and hence bends back to resource base which is depleted by the Capital. With a depleted resource base, as the operation of the Indian Capital cannot extend beyond production of one-time-surplus, NEI depends on Indian Capital to enter into the processes of continuous production of surplus which gets curtailed in the flight of resources from NEI. Therefore, the logic of metropolitan Indian Capital does not allow a full entry of NEI in the Indian market as it leads to a backward bending of surplus into extractions from depleted resource bases. The non-capitalist modes of production in NEI remains away from either the production or extraction of surplus yet it suffers this moment of Capital's bending backward to the depleted resource base. In such a situation there would be a slump in the development of productive forces and a steady depletion of resources leading to an inchoate inclusion of NEI within the Indian market. This situation jibes well with the logic of surplus extraction that leaves off the periphery as a residue. Fortunately, NEI as the residue of surplus extraction finds itself disjointed from extended reproduction of Capital as it happens in the core of the economy. Left to itself there is recyclable sector of domestic and peripheral economy existing in parallel with the intermediary sectors that exists as the periphery of reproduction of Capital and the core Indian market always providing an access of the Indian Capital to the primary sectors of economy. This foray of Indian Capital into the primary sector as an extended reproduction of Indian Capital subordinates the primary sector to the intermediate. But this subordination and foray of Indian Capital notwithstanding, there is no extended reproduction of resources from NEI and hence NEI cannot contribute to reproduction of Capital. One can clearly observe the dichotomy between the foray of Indian Capital and the limited entry of NEI into the Indian market, which results into an unhindered access to the resource base of NEI while such resources are only depleted. The reverse and backward entry of Indian Capital into the resource base of NEI leaves the residue of resources and the primary sectors of the economy by dampening the productive forces in those sectors. Further, the development of intermediary mode of production in a backward extension of the Indian market from the core to the periphery jibes well with peripherialization of the domestic mode of production as extraction of surplus from the resource base could be maintained by the backward extension of Capital reproduced at the core of India's economy which simultaneously keeps NEI as a periphery and makes the entry of Indian Capital possible in NEI.

What emerges from the foregoing discussion is the non-reproducibility of resources from NEI that ironically sustains the backward extension of Indian Capital as well as an intermediary domain of production that maintains a linkage between the core and the periphery. Such an intermediary domain becomes the site of dominant Capitalist development, as it must move within the trajectory of core-periphery relationship. This overarching framework of core-periphery relationship does not allow the integration of periphery with the core, as this would jeopardize the processes of surplus extraction. Therefore, perpetuation of periphery and development of an intermediary market as an extension of the core by its vary operation limit development only with intermediary modes of production. At a certain phase of development of the intermediary mode of production, development could be sustained only if the backward extension of core is supplemented by extractions from the domestic and the peripheral. Such an extraction at the local level is meant to provide fulcrum to the processes of surplus generation that moves from the periphery to the core. Local extractions results into destruction of peripheral modes of production and at a certain stage of accentuated destruction of the localized modes of production, intermediary sectors of the economy fully gain an access and control over the resource base of peripheral modes of production. Such access to the peripheral by the intermediary destroys the residual spaces of production and eats into the autonomy of local modes of production. As development operates within such core-periphery logic it results into usurpation of domestic modes of production and a complete destruction of community based resources.

As development operates through reproduction of relations of production in the form of core-periphery relations, the greater backward extension of the market of the core and its consequent subsumption of the domestic, the stronger is the effect of surplus extraction. The effect is realized in the form of a periphery becoming just a market for goods and services brought by the core, which develops into a complete subsumption of the productive forces of the periphery. This kind of development coheres with the usual modes of development that presents the periphery as underdeveloped in comparison to the potential of the core. But the paradox is that core develops and spreads underdevelopment by way of a direct exploitation of the periphery. Space is ordered by processes of development in such a way that core-peripheral relationship is sustained. It is for this reason that hill spaces of NEI practice a subsistence form of economy while plains as an extension of markets of the mainland follow an economy of surplus and abundance. Hill spaces are marked by underdeveloped productive forces while plains and valleys are marked by productive forces of the core. Therefore, plains become the centres of economic activities while hills remain the outside the pale of the market in terms of production. Nevertheless, hills become the site of marketing products from the plains and such marketing is possible provided resources in the hills are controlled and owned by producers who have a foothold in the plains. This dichotomy between the hills and the plains in terms of spatial configurations marks the asymmetric production relations, which is sustained and perpetuated by the development of market forces under capitalism. It is to be remembered that development acts as an agency of reproduction of relations of production and in the context of center-periphery relationship development follows the logic of the centre. Resisting paradigms of development, therefore, tries to subvert the capitalist relations of production. In the context of NEI such a resistance arises from the underdeveloped productive forces themselves as forces of domestic and peripheral modes of production mobilize collectivities against the market, most often a backward extension of the core. Such collectivities gain strength, as there is an expansion of periphery in spaces where communities lived in a self-reliant manner as such peripheries are steadily appropriated by the intermediary modes of production that the collectivities develop by the possibility of aligning with elites who become a part of the expansionist process of market formations. But economic forces cannot alone align and subsume domestic modes of production under intermediate and capitalist modes of production. It is rather a number of mediating agencies that determine the limits of the subsumption of the domestic within the intermediary. The state plays a crucial role in regulating the processes of subsumption and remains an observer. The domain of the operation of the State is overshadowed by backward extension of the core and hence its mediating role gets limited to facilitation of the expansion of the intermediaries and bridging up the gap between the domestic, intermediary and the capitalist modes of production. The crucial question is does the state merely follow the market and act as a peripheral entity within the framework of center-periphery relations?

Although, state as an actor is constrained, communities located in peripheries enter into the contradictory relationship between intermediary and domestic and intermediary and capitalist. Such contradictory relationship acts as a source of putting ones own situation and ones place within relations of production as a countervailing force to the processes of appropriation.

As in the peripherialization of the economy the peripheral groups establish a new language of articulation of their identity and their sense of distinctness drives them towards assuming a specific discursive identity against the dominant currents of appropriation. Identity stands beside their ontological grounds as if they are interpellated in the process of subsumption of the weaker modes of production by the dominant. The weaker modes of production become the site for colonization resulting into resistant identities to the force of colonization. In the case of NEI such resistant identities exists in relation to subsumption of the weaker modes of production by the dominant. Interpellation of such identities indeed marks a kind of cultural identification of peripheries, which are simultaneously lying inside and outside of the mainstream processes of nation building. A cursory look into struggles over linguistic, ethnic and cultural rights assume a form of preservation of self-identity that is juxtaposed over and against the movements within the processes of subsumption of one mode of production by the other.

The concept of assertion of an identity take it's meaning from the constraining and enabling structure of centre-periphery relationship. In the context of NEI identities develop as an exercise of agency in the cases of appropriation of a mode of production that renders social groups excluded from the structure of reward and recognition. As a result identities can be, at the same time both the subordinate object of the hierarchical relations of production given rise to by centre-periphery relations and subjects who are agents in their own lives, capable of exercising power in the generative sense of self-actualization. Therefore, the production of identities follow a trajectory of resisting the top down process of appropriation as also subvert the backward extension of the dominant modes of production. Although development processes attempt at reincorporating the agency of the subsumed subjects in it's trickling down effects such that subjects do not threaten to dislodge the very process of subsumption and appropriation. This subversion assumes a form of struggle between the dominant and the non-dominant forms of identities, especially a crisis of identity is generated in the extended claims of pan-Indian identity geared up by smaller nationalities of NEI against the State sponsored nationalism. Within the larger context of political economy of underdevelopment, smaller nationalities assume a potential of building up a class orientation that cuts across the modalities of appropriation and thereby occupy a distinct position within the developmental ensemble that comprises of modes of production, space and modes of development. Such an agency of smaller nationalities and their class alliances negotiated the structural rules of reproduction in favour of their own collective identities. In the pubic space such alliances drew the line between the state and the people and exercised the capability of reconstruction of the social space. Such a reconstruction is possible if identities can transgress the imposing fòrces of economic and social appropriation and secure a place within the movements of Capital and attain a visible position within the configuration of development. But this is possible only through resisting from the position of a weaker mode of production that gets appropriated into intermediary and thereby forcing a configuration of a resisting identity, a bottom up process where identities exercise their agency beside the hierarchical relations of production. Such exercise of agency assumes a trajectory of politics that determines the economic processes and in turn gets determined by those processes.

Instead of merely emphasizing a role for the non-economic forces in social life, what could be pursued is an integrated process of changes in the mode of production resulting into changes in spatial reconfiguration of modes of production, which further gets related to the internal conflicts between modes of production affecting modes of development or social relations of production that work for establishing dominance over the weaker modes. Non-economic forces such as cultural identities occupy a place within these processes of internal shifts and changes between modes of production and development and any autonomous moves in the sphere of the non-economic contextualizes itself within these shifts between economic forces. The specific causal-nomological connection that arises out of the interrelationship between the sphere of the economic and the non-economic evolves onto the conflicts and resistances endemic in the structural relations of production and affect them in a definite manner without any predeterminations.

As the non-economic factor, Ethnicity assumes universality in the context of NEI and puts forth a principle of individuation of communities that bases it upon the trajectory of politics. This further develops into a program of conserving the essential cultural markers as well as establishing a comparative normative superiority over others to open up a process of construction, contest and conflict. The concrete politics of articulation of specificity of ethnic communities involve constructing an ethnic domain and establishing a normative privilege over others. Therefore articulation of ethnicity stretches beyond the specific domain of the ethnic in its attempt to establish a normative superiority and spills over into larger public space in which it engages in a contest for priority of its ethnocentric position. Such a process is evident in the construction of major ethnic identities like *Assamese*, *Naga* and *Mizo* in the domain of the public by a selective mobilization of history and culture that distinguish them from others. This domain of public assumes a certain character by virtue of an already existent order in which communities are often intermingled, overlapped and crisscrossed in their specific articulation. The case of overlapping between *Naga* tribes and *Manipuris* and *Kukis* in Manipur created demands for a new construction of territories. In case of *Bodos* demand to create a Bodo Council or a State out of the mixed populace of Assam created an exclusive ethnic claim for rendering the presence of others irrelevant. Thereby the public space in NEI remains in a state of flux in which determination of normative position is affected by agencies that are supposedly neutral, such as the State. The role of the State contributes to determination and positioning of ethnocentric points of view that remain directed towards the other in a manner that mellows down specificities in a site of multiple claims, as the State aims at management of communities. Often it persuades a kind of homogeneity between communities to pass it as serving the interest of all. Therefore State presents a minimal ethnocentricity mixed with an other-directed approach that often neutralizes specificities in the normative limits drawn by the State. Within such an instrumental working of the public space and civil society as delimited by the State, the ethnic life world is often squeezed to worlds of self representation, which as a phenomenon is a kind of reification or decontextualization that only herald contestation with other to the extent of mutual annihilation.

The crucial question is, do such contests secure the cultural, political and economic rights of communities? Or violence generated through such a politics of contest in the instrumental public space act as a source of attenuation of identities? Can an ethnic community resist dominance of other by turning violent within the public space? Such questions go along with the politics of development played in the negotiation between the state and the communities, which further base itself upon the structural relations of production and how these relations shape the construction of identities in the public space. As an example, the claim of *Bodos* to be different than the Assamese involve contest over intermediary sites of production, as market expands itself in the areas dominated by *Bodos* and displaces their traditional modes of production. Displacement of traditional economic practices by the market forces and decontextualization of the tribal mores of life by the operation of civil society and state result into an identity crisis, a sense of loss, propelled by which the weaker identity asserts itself against its others. But such an assertion is fraught with the limits drawn by the politics of development and the emerging mode of production. Such new forms of social forces take dominating role, these act as leveler of differences and compels the communities to assert their self-conscious sense of being different. One can surmise that such assertions of difference mark changes in the pattern of dominance, especially when the traditional mode of production suffers a kind of subsumption.

One can further go into the modalities of constitution of ethnic in the processes of Development. Taking ethnic identity as a given, articulation of identity intervenes in the public space to evolve autonomy. Response of other will largely determine how it further presents itself in the fructuous space of the public. Taking ethnic identity as constructed, its internal search for homogeneity often takes the form of strong articulation against others, because without a perceived hegemonic other such constructions remain weak. This articulation against a hegemonic other again brings back mutually reinforcing polarities within itself: one, how much ground the ethnic community can acquire in a field of co-existence with other and secondly how much it can resist other. This two polarities often run at cross-purposes to make either the process of ethnic fragmentation more visible or to show that in relation to the dominant ethnic groups, they remain marginalized. This is a strange mode of decentering the ethnic identity in the presence of stronger other and hence their autonomy always remains under a threat.

Within a certain modality of reciprocation and recognition it is possible for an ethnic identity to assert its autonomy in terms of certain inalienable cultural, political and economic rights. But these modalities of reciprocation and recognition involve a mutual sharing of perspective, position and power, which obviously is determined through a tedious process of negotiation. Such a process being largely political leaves open the scope of non-mitigation of ethnic aspiration. Mitigation is totally conditional in a situation when others are not ready to recognize rightful claims of a community. What is demanded of an ethnicity in despair is an act of reciprocation to other before its voice is listened to. In the domain of the public, redressal and mitigation of ethnic aspiration is placed at a secondary level, instead what is given primary significance is a community conforming to the normative order of the State. Therefore the claims of autonomy of ethnic communities are normalized within public space and within the framework of accommodations with other communities. What is given primary importance is the acceptance of the normative order by an ethnic community and not adherence to its own life-world norms and institutions. A liberal democracy accommodates an ethnic community with all its life world institutions and attempts at allowing it a free function. All this is done to ensure a complete and total absorption of ethnic communities inside the mechanisms of State, Development and public space.

Two important question could be raised in this context: one, does such a mechanism guarantee the autonomous existence of ethnic community or it merely makes it a part to a whole; secondly does the apparent leveling of specificities of ethnic communities ensure a free and smooth inter-ethnic relation or it merely implicates the processes of reciprocation and recognition? Especially if one goes into the specific mooring of an ethnic community as given and also takes into account its articulation/discourses or trace its relations with other in terms of reciprocation and recognition the exteriority that it produces give it a certain modality. If the exteriority of such articulations end up in enhanced contestation there would arise a greater sensitivity in its articulation always running against its own grain and thereby turning it into a narrowly ethnocentric discourse intolerant to both members within and the other outside. Shifts of this nature that make an identity volatile acquire greater visibility and correspondingly shifts in political articulation would bring about an attempt to dominate. Such constrained and internally generated resistance goes onto turning violent and there is a rise in those forms of action that violate the existence of other. Ethnic discourses bearing experiences of wounds and deprivation turn into a mode of self assertion directed towards other often violating their existence. Any mediation in such cases resort to an involuntary digging up of ethnic perspective and thereby resulting into a further round of sensitivity.

The crucial question here again is how could one distinguish an articulation of life world norms from sensitized responses? If ethnic identity assumes a kind of autonomy within itself to contextualize its articulation but contextualization of itself could never completely be fixed upon stable other. Mutual processes of reciprocation and recognition keep on fracturing the inside of ethnic discourses to reshape it in a different from. While longing for fraternity in its contextualized articulation of identity, the play of changing relationship with other often ends up with disruptions, further resulting into directedness towards other.

Apart from these other-directed struggles, the ethnic groups effect mobilizations by drawing upon the 'authentic and autonomous' cultural symbols and ethnic specificity that are apparently different to that of the groups they contest. This contestation was initially premised on anthropological markers separating the Mongolian groups (the *Nagas*, *Mizos*, *Meiteis*, the *Ahoms* etc.) from the non-Mongolian communities who inhabit the other parts of India. Today this mobilization and contestation is premised more innocuously on ethnicity and cultural difference. While the mobilizational pattern is similar in that they legitimize their movements upon claims of authenticity, many (for example the Naga/Kuki; Bodo/Santhal) of these conflicts are said to be a resistance against asymmetrical division of power between dominant and weaker groups and cannot be explained solely in terms of authenticity. Such asymmetries have their roots in the asymmetries of modes of development.

The recognition of ethnic groups through ethno-linguistic federal units has to a considerable extent shaped the post-colonial Indian State and defined ethnic identity along these ethno-linguistic territorial markers in the region. This coupled with the 'labeling process' by which the state recognizes an ethnic group defines the hierarchical status and resource shares of ethnic groups. Thus Manipur is for *Manipuris*, Assam for *Assamese*, and Nagaland for *Nagas* etc. This has also simultaneously produced an externalization whereby the identity of

Assamese, *Manipuri* or *Naga* is contested. Though most of these states consist of one or more dominant ethnic groups, they are however, not mono ethno-federal entities in the sense where membership is restricted to only one ethnic group within the concerned state. Despite the adherence to the principle of linguistic and ethnic homogeneity in the reorganization of the states, members of one ethnic community even today constitute a substantial majority in the territorial jurisdiction of another. For example the 'Nagas' a dominant ethnic group of Nagaland constitute a substantial majority in Manipur. This presence has often led to claims about the arbitrary demarcation of state boundaries without respect to the historical claims of the various ethnic groups resulting in political and insurgent contestation. Thus contestations and claims in the region often reflected in armed confrontations assume a territorial character and clearly identifiable zones of conflict.

Interestingly at another level some sections of the dominant groups reflecting their grievances against the Indian State are engaged in an armed confrontation with it. The claim even in this case is the difference of the groups in terms of culture and history with that of mainland India. Consequently there is the emergence of stratified levels of conflict where the claims are legitimated on similar premises of difference but follows rhetoric of claim-making that contests the claims of the group against which it is being made. In other words most of these conflicts and claims despite mutually contesting are united in their contestation of the political legitimacy of the Indian State over the region. The resulting inter-locking web of confrontation and conflicts, based on difference of claims and culture has led to the stifling of not only the democratic space in its institutional form but also any substantive normative standard between the conflicting groups. Consequently despite legitimization of the claims by the involved groups as democratic aspirations and democratic right to self-determination, democracy as a principle for negotiating intra and inter group differences remains a far cry.

Consequently, all these states in varying degrees of intensity confront armed struggles by ethnic groups who not only question the arbitrary consolidation of ethnic groups into states but also question their integration with the Indian State. This has resulted in the emergence of conflict zones in the entire region where various ethnic groups are engaged in armed confrontation at two different levels—with the state of India and with the other ethnic groups. In a sense ethnic identity in the region operates both as a 'structure' and as an 'agency' that mediate and regulate social relationships and processes in which the politics of difference is communicated and reinforced.

Scholarly investigations of the motivational forces responsible for the emergence of renewed emphasis and claims based on ethnic authenticity and the resulting conflicts can be posited along a spectrum of theoretical debates. While some accounted at it as a reaction to the hegemonization and standardization of a grand narrative either by the Indian State or by the dominant ethnic groups, others have assessed them as the result of the emergence of a new 'indigenous' group of political entrepreneurs who manipulate existing ethnic fault-lines for reconfiguration of the power relations and economic production. Still others locate the rationale of the insurgencies as a subaltern project that attempts to recover the consciousness of the mobilized masses and historical personality that justifies their often exclusive and insular claims.

However, though most of these accounts are a post facto analysis of the 'why' of ethnic resurgence none of these theoretical assessments addresses the issue of the "boundary processes" in identity construction. This account is necessary because without understanding the processes of ethnic self [and other] constructions that define and structure the development of group-consciousness and identity, it would be difficult to assess the present ethnic imbroglio in the region. Since if we are to understand why some groups are '[re] inventing' their own 'indigenous' space away from their earlier affiliations. Therefore, the way collective memories are based on an insular perception of the narratives of the past are utilized to construct collective selves and structure collective identity movements have to be properly recorded. The historical traditions that fortify a sequenced history leading to the emergence and collective sharing of group-identity; the social, political, economic, and cultural processes at work help to maintain or re-discover ethnic differences and finally the forces that mediate this consciousness and effect its convergence into a movement constitute the contemporary turbulence through which the region is undergoing.

Glossary

Accumulation: Accumulation connotes not only relationship between production and capitalization of surplus value but also a relationship of reproduction.

Agrarian Reform: Distribution of land to needy peasants, as well as government support programs that are necessary to make beneficiaries economically viable.

Appropriation: Appropriating is appropriation of surplus generated by capital-labour-commodity relationship obtained in a mode of production. Surplus is appropriated by an attendant exchange relation.

Base and Superstructure: Marx and Engel use the building-like metaphor of base and superstructure to propound the idea that the economic structure of society i.e.' the base' conditions the existence and forms of State and social consciousness i.e. the 'superstructure'.

Bourgeoisie: A Marxist term for those who own society's productive resources.

Capital-intensive production: Industrial or agricultural production that relies heavily on machinery and technology rather than human factor.

Colonization: Asserting control over a previously independent region. Marxist analysis of colonialism has approached it by focusing on several general views. First, they have tried to establish that direct political control of non-capitalist societies was in some way a result of reproductive requirements or tendential developments of European and American industrial capitalist economies in the 19th century. Second, they have examined, the political, economic and ideological effects of industrial capitalist entry into non-capitalist societies. In this they have been primarily concerned with the results of these effects for development of socialism in both the industrial capitalist and colonized societies; consequently, they have tended to focus on the forms of colonial capitalist development created and perpetuated by the colonizing powers, and on the implications of this. Finally, they have assessed the possible consequences of socialist development in colonial societies for socialist transformation in colonizing countries.

Commercialization of Agriculture: The process whereby subsistence farmers (i.e. those raising largely for their own family consumption) convert sometime unwillingly, to farming for the commercial market.

Contradiction: contradiction although is used as a metaphor it assumes a distinctive meaning in Marxist literature in the case of human where it specifies any situation which allows the satisfaction of one end only at the cost of another, i.e. bind or constant.

Critical Geography: It is an approach rather than a theoretical system; "critical geography" is a project, which has two prominent dimensions. First, it seeks to deconstruct the tradition of geographical thought as it has been represented in various intellectual histories within the discipline of Geography. "Critical geography" brings the "methods" of post-structuralist historiography to analyze how geography emerged as a mode of analysis in the late nineteenth century and how a tradition came to be created around it. As a form of revisionist historiography, "critical geography" is part of a general intellectual movement within Geography to re-evaluate the history and key intellectuals of the discipline. Secondly, "critical geography" seeks to displace conventional understandings of the geographical in global politics.

Determination: Marxists explain things by finding what determines what. There are two notions within it. The first is that determination is a matter of antecedents, stimulating, generating, or providing the occasion for consequences. The second one is that determination is a matter of the nature of wholes making possible relations within them.

Developmental State: A state that intervenes actively in the economy in order to guide or promote particular economic development goals such as full employment.

Dominance: Dominance is conceived, as the superiority of one of at least two mutually constituted entities that are apparently equal in status but is ordered in a hierarchy. This hierarchical form of ordering produces relationship of the dominant and the non-dominant. Dominance, therefore, signifies the dialectical privilege of one the two interrelated entities, which together constitute a system of production/ rule etc. Also dominance is understood in terms of what is being dominated i.e. the non-dominant factors of a system of production. Dominance is further understood in symbolic terms, when the apparent equality between the at least two constitutive elements relapses into an inequality of relation such that one of the two constitute the other in a kind of displacement. Similarly, it is also possible that one of the two appropriates the other that would signify a surplus of meaning in the one, which appropriates and thereby would neutralize the place of the other.

Exchange: According to Marxian theory Exchange is the most immediate economic relation under capitalism. All individuals of all classes necessarily participate in exchange. But exchange is only a moment in the circulation of capital as a whole.

Expropriation: It has the double meaning of what is left as a residue after extraction of surplus in a given mode of production as well surplus that precedes appropriation. Therefore, it connotes the process of appropriation with reference to the mode and method of appropriation.

Extended Reproduction: It connotes accumulation where a given fraction of the total surplus value is employed to purchase additional capital, variable and constant in order to increase the existing scale of production.

Forces and Relations of Production: Forces/Relations of Production lies underneath in any society's mode of production. The Productive forces conceived by Marx include means of production and labour power. Relations of production are constituted by the economic ownership of production of forces; under capitalism the most fundamental of these relations is the bourgeoisie's ownership of means of production while proletariat owns only its labour power.

Hats: Rural market places in the NEI region where the locally produced commodities are sold.

Hegemony: It is composed of two diametrically opposed senses: first the meaning of domination as in 'hegemonism' and secondly, to mean leadership, implying some notion of consent. In Marxian sense Gramsci's notion of Hegemony i.e. the system of alliances which the working class must create to overthrow the bourgeoisie state and to serve as the social basis of the workers' state, is used.

Historical Dialectic: A Marxist term used to describe the ongoing tension between particular forces of history.

Informal Sector: The part of t he economy that is unregulated by the government or society while similar activates are regulated and taxed.

Jhumming: It's a kind of shifting cultivation practised by most of tribal communities in NEI. This principal mode of agricultural land involves the clearing of land for cultivation and rotation of the agricultural field throughout different time period.

Labour Power: The capacity to do useful work, which adds Value to commodities. It is labour power that workers sell to capitalists for money wage.

Labour Process: It is the process whereby labour is materialized or objectified in use values.

Liberalization of the Economy: Reducing the degree of state intervention in the economy (referring to the 18th century classical liberalism of Adam Smith).

Mass Mobilization: The process whereby large segments of the population become activated politically. Governments or revolutionary movements may choose to mobilize the population.

Mediation: It refers to establishing connections by means of some intermediary.

Middle Class: The term 'middle class' is used in various ways in Marx and Engels. It refers to a class, which is a part of the possessing class differentiated from aristocracy. Marx used the term more in the sense of 'petty bourgeoisie' to designate the class and strata between bourgeoisie and the working class. The development of middle class is taken as an important feature of capitalist development.

Mode of Production: It does not have a single consistent sense in the Marxian language. However, it is generally understood as the ensemble of social relations of production, which constitutes the economic structure of any society.

Mode of Development: Development understood in a given or an emergent mode involves identification of an essential feature of development. Following the logic of mode of production each of the mode of production causes a level of development, which could be characterized through a definite achievement of a particular social formation. As development is a dynamic process, modes of development could be understood in terms of crucial relation that characterizes transition/movement from a certain stage of development to another. For example how market relation produce development could be conceived as a stage of development, which is related to non-market relations as well as to, advanced stages of development.

Nationality: A population with its own language, cultural traditions and historical aspirations that frequently claim sovereignty over a particular territory.

Non-Capitalist Mode of Production: Non-Capitalist Mode of Production includes post-capitalist societies, which are concerned with those social systems that are pre-capitalist. This means that the existence of the pre-capitalist with the capitalist modes of production historically precede the full development of capitalism in a social formation, though it is contemporaneous with capitalism on a world scale. The dialectic of development involves non-capitalist formations as the source of mutual negation, while the negation does not take a complete form. Rather it produces the possibility of co-existence and co-extension between two modes of production that are supposed to be mutually exclusive and thereby giving rise to a hybrid space of production and the blocked dialectic between the two.

Peasantry: The term generally refers to those who labour on the land and posses their means of production: tools and the land itself. The dispossed peasantry, of course, is a social reality.

Periphery: Third World countries, commonly seen by dependency theorists as occupying a lesser rank in the international economy.

Praxis: Refers in general to action, activity; and in Marx's sense to the free, universal, creative and self-creative activity through which man creates (makes produces) and changes (shapes) his historical, human world himself; an activity specific to man, through which he is basically differentiated from other beings.

Primitive Mode of Production: In this type of accumulation means of production is owned by the community and surplus is also consumed within the community itself. Absence of market and class differentiation is a characteristic of such mode of production.

Reification: The act (or result of the act) of transforming human properties, relations and actions of man-produced things which have become independent (and which are imagined as originally independent) of man and govern his life. Also transformations of human beings into things-like beings which do not behave in a human way but according to the laws of the thing-world.

Relative Deprivation: The gap between and individual or group's expectations or desires and their actual development.

Reproduction: Reproduction involves both production and the setting up of conditions whereby production can continue to take place. Marx divides reproduction into simple reproduction and extended reproduction.

State: In Marxist thought State is regarded as the institutions beyond all others whose function is to maintain and define class domination and exploitation. The classical Marxist views modern State as a committee for managing the common affairs of the whole bourgeoisie. The State is viewed as an instrument of ruling class designated by the virtue of its ownership and control of means of production.

Structure and Structural Relations of Production: Structures are not directly observable relations but levels of reality of the functioning, which constitutes the deeper logic of a social system. Marx regarded a social formation as the historical production of a mode of production. Any mode of production gives rise to a set of objective relations that involves a number of social, institutional, economic and cultural factors that govern the operation of any mode of production. Structural relations of production includes the whole ensemble of social relation that emerge out of a given mode of production and it is through that a structure continues to function.

Surplus value: The extraction of the surplus is the specific way of exploitation that takes place under capitalism, the *differntia specifica* of the capitalist modes production, in which the surplus takes the form of profit, and exploitation results from the working class producing a net product which can be sold for than they receive as wages.

Traditional Society: Societies that adhere to long-standing values and customs that have been extensively transformed by modernization.

Tribe: Marginalized and colonized social groups that share a collective identity and language and believe in common myths and customary practices with a distinct social organization based on kinship relationship.

Underconsumption: a situation where a short fall of demand for consumption goods arises and persists due to systemic tendencies. It is advanced as a cause of periodic crisis as well as a chronic tendency toward overproduction and stagnation in capitalist economies.

Underdevelopment: the theory founded on the notions of economic surplus, and the generation of absorption of this surplus within the capitalist economy. The major tenet of under-development theory is that the reproductive requirements of the industrial capitalist economies impose a sectorally uneven capitalist development, which restricts the potential growth of the domestic economy.

Uneven Development: Under capitalism it is the possibility of overtaking competitors in the use of up-to-date production technique and or labour organization, i.e. enjoying a higher productivity of labour, which determines the rhythm of development of .both form and of nations.

Bibliography

Acharya, S.K. (1998). "Ethnic Processes in the North-Eastern India", *Economic and Political Weekly*, 21 May, pp. 1068-1077.

Adorno, Theodor W. (1990). *Negative Dialectics*, Translated by E.B. Ashton, Routledge, London.

Agnew, J. (1987). *Place and Politics: The Geographical Mediation of State and Society*, Allen and Unwin, Boston.

Agnew, J. (1993). "Representing Space: Space, Scale and Culture in Social Science" in Duncan, J and Ley, D (edit.). *Place/Culture/ Representation*, pp.251-271, Routledge, London.

Aijaz, R. (1998). "Correcting Educational Imbalances of North-Eastern Region", *Yojana*, 16-30 April, pp 22-24.

Akoijam, A.Binod and Oinam B. (2002). "Eighth Assembly Election in Manipur: Beyond the Discursive Verdict of a Fragmented Kind", in www.manipuronline.com, May.

Alam,K.(1983). *The Economic Development of Assam*, Gauhati University Press, Guahati.

Alavi, H. (1975). "India and the Colonial Mode of Production", *Economic and Political Weekly*, Special Number, August, pp. 1235-1262.

Althusser, L (1970). "Ideology and Ideological State Apparatuses", reprinted in Althusser, L(ed)., *Lenin and Philosophy and Other Essays*, NLB and Sheed and Ward,1971,London.

Amin, S. (1977). *Imperialism and Unequal Development*, Monthly Review Press, New York.

Amin, S. (2000). *Specters of Capitalism: A Critique to Current Intellectual Fashion*, Monthly Review Press, New York.

Anderson, B. (1991). *Imagined Communities: Reflections on the Origin and Spread of Nationalism* (revised edition), Verso, London.

Bagchi, A.K.(1988). "Colonialism and the Nature of Capitalist Enterprise In India", *Economic and Political Weekly*, 30 July, pp. PE38-PE50..

Bahadur, M. (2000). *Tribal Hand woven Fabrics of Manipur*, Mutua Museam, *Imphal.*

Baishya, P. (1972). "Silk Industries in an Assam Town: Its Problems and Prospects", *Yojana*, 1 August, pp. 557-558.

Banerjee, P, et al. (1999). "Indo-Bangladesh Cross-Border Migration and Trade", *Economic and Political Weekly*, 4th September.

Banerjee-Guha, S. (1992). "Geography of Political Economy: Some Understanding in India", *National Geographical Journal of India*, vol.38,pp 129-136.

Banerjee-Guha, S. (2002). "Critical Geographical Praxis: Globalization and Socio-Spatial Disorder", *Economic and Political Weekly*, 2-9th November, www.epw.org.in

Bardhan, P.K. (1984). *Political economy of Development in India*, OUP, New Delhi.

Baru, S. (1983). "Karl Marx and the Indian Society", *Economic and Political Weekly"*, 10 December, pp2102-2108.

Baruah, A.K. (1989) *Social Tensions in Assam*, Purbanchal Prakashan, Gauhati.

Baruah, S. (1986). "Lessons of Assam", *Economic and Political Weekly*, 15th February, pp. 282-284.

Baruah, S. (1989). "Minority Policy in the North-East: Achievement and Dangers", *Economic and Political Weekly*, 16 September, pp. 2087-290.

Baruah, S. (1999). *India Against Itself: Assam and the Politics of Sulenatrination*, University of Pennsylvania Press, Philadelphia.

Baruah, S. (2000). "Clash of Resource Regimes in Colonial Assam: A Nineteenth-Century Puzzle Revisited", *Journal of Peasant Studies*, vol.28, no.1 (October), pp.108-124.

Baruah, S. (2002), "Gulliver's Trouble and Militants in North-East India", *Economic and Political Weekly*, 12th October, www.epw.org.in

Bensman, J and Lilienfeld, R. (1973). *Craft and Consciousness: Occupational Technique and the Development of World Images*, John Wiley and Sons, New York.

Bernstein, H. (ed) (1973). *Underdevelopment and Development: The Third World Today*, Penguin Publication, London.

Bezbaruah, M.P. (2001). "Tourism in North-East India", *Dialogue*, Vol.2, No.4, April-June.

Bezbaruah, M.P. (2001). "Creation of Smaller States and Economic Progress in India's North-Eastern Region", *Dialogue*, Vol.2, No.3, January-March.

Bharadwaj, K. (1982). "Regional Differentiation in India: A Note", *Economic and Political Weekly*", Annual Number-April, pp. 605-614.

Bhattacharjee, J.B. (1989). *Sequences of Development in North-East India*, Omsons Publisher, New Delhi.

Bhattacharjee, P.R. (1985). "Regional Planning For North-East India" in Alam, K (edit.) Planning in the North Eastern India, pp.233-241. Omsons Publications, Guwahati.

Bhowmik, S. (1985). "Plantation Labour in North-East India", *Economic and Political Weekly*, 30 March, pp.538-541

Bhuyan, S.H et.al (1990). "Market and Regulated Market?, the case of Assam, India", *HSD Monograph* No.19, Asian Institute of Technology, Bangkok, Thailand.

Biswas, P. (1997). The Counterhegemonic Struggles and the New Social Movements in North-East India, *Window, Journal of Shillong Study Circle*, Vol. 5., December.

Biswas, P . (2001). "The Outsider, the State and Nation From Below North-East India as Subject of Exclusion" in Kausar Azam(ed) (2001), *Ethnicity, Identity and the State in South Asia*, South Asian Publishers Ltd., New Delhi.

Biswas, P. and Suklabaidya, C. (2004) *Ethnophilosophy: Understanding North-East India*, Samya, Kolkata (Forthcoming).

Black, J.K. (1991). *Development in Theory and Practice*, Westview Press, Oxford.

Bourdieu, P. (1989). "Social Space and Symbolic Power", *Sociological Theory*, 79(1), pp.18-26.

Burton, F and Carlen, P. (1979). *Official Discourse: On Discourse Analysis, Government Publications, Ideology and the State*,

Routledge and Kegan Paul, London.

Butola B. S. (1996). "Sublimation of Identities in North east India" in North East India History Association Proceedings, Session 16, New Delhi :ICHR pp. 223-236.

Butola B. S. (1997). "Deconstructing Poverty in North east India" in B.Dutta Roy et.al. (ed.) *Population, Poverty and Environment in North east India*, Specturm Publications, New Delhi.pp. 187-202.

Butola B. S. (1998). "Nation States, Modernity and the Indian Context" in *North Eastern Hill University Journal of Humanities and Social sciences,* Vol.8.No.1pp.124-138.

Butola B. S. (2002). "Human Rights and Nationalized Civilizations" in Ranju R.Dhamala et.al.(ed.) *Human Rights and Insurgence: The North East India,* Shipra Publications, New Delhi.pp.163-178.

Chakravarty, A.K. and Chopra, R.C. (1977). "Prospects for Growth of Electronics Industry in Hill Areas with Special Reference to North-Eastern Region", *Yojana*, 26 January, pp. 125-135.

Choudhury A. (1996). "Ethnogenesis in North east India"in M.M.Agrawal (ed*.) Ethnicity, Culture and nationalism in North East India*, Indus Publishing Company, New Delhi. pp.123-35.

Choudhury, D. (1998). "Conserving Genetic Heterogeneity in North east India" in M K Raha et.al. (edit.)*North east India: The Human Interface*, Commonwealth Publishers, New Delhi.

Collins, R. (1990). "Changing Conceptions in the Sociology of Professions" in Torstendahl, R and Burrage, M (edit.) *Knowledge, State and Stragety*, pp.11-23, Sage Publications, London.

Dandekar, C. (1990). *Surveillance, Power and Modernity, Polity Press*, Cambridge.

Dasgupta, D.etal. (2000), "Growth and Interstate Disparities In India", *Economic and Political Weekly*, 1 July, pp. 2413-2422.

Dasgupta, K. (1983). "Plantation Economy and Land Tenure System in Brahmaputra Valley 1839-1914", *Economic and Political Weekly*, 16 July, pp. 1280-1290.

Datta, P.S. (1990). "Roots of Insurgency", *Seminar*, No.366, pp. 47-49.

Dawar, J. (1996). "The Symbolic of Mishmi Identity" in *North East*

India History Association Proceedings, Session 16,ICHR New Delhi

Dawar, J (1997). "A Bourdieuian Insight into Symbolic to Reality in Mishmi Imageries", *North East India History Association Proceedings*, Session 17, ICHR.

de Certeau, M.(1984). *The Practice of Everyday Life*, University of California Press, California.

Dev, R. (1995). "Traditional Political Institutions in Meghalaya: A Critique of Ethnocentrism" in *North East India Political Science Association*, 3rd Annual Session, Shillong. pp.67-78.

Dev, R (2001). "Identity Claims: Paradox of Recognition and Redistribution in North East India" in Kousar Azam (ed.) *Ethnicity, Identity and State in South Asia*, South Asian Publishers, New Delhi. pp.221-31.

Dhar, P.K. (2001). *The Economy of Assam,* Kalyani Publishers, Guahati.

Dholakia, R.H. (1994). "Spatial Dimensions of Acceleration of Economic Growth In India", *Economic and Political Weekly*, 27 August, pp.2303-2309.

Dikshit, R.D (1971). "Geography and Federalism", *Annals of Association of American Geographers*, Vol.61, No.1, pp 97-115.

Driver, F. (1992). "Geography's Empire: Histories of Geographical Knowledge", *Environment and Planning D: Society and Space*, 10(1), pp.23-40.

Duggal, R., Verma, R., Mathew, S.A., (1999) "Nagaland Issues in Governance" in *Economic Political Weekly,* Dec, 11-17.

Elwin, V. (1964 2nd edtn.). *A Philosophy for NEFA*, North East Frontier Agency, Shillong.

Elwin, V. (1977). *The Myths of North East Frontier of India*, Govt. of Arunachal Pradesh Publications, Itanagar.

Entrikin, N. (1994). "Place and Region", *Progress in Human Geography*, 18(2), pp.227-233.

Fernandes, W. (2001) "Missionaries and Tribal Identities in North east India: A Historical Perspective", *Economic and Political Weekly*, 6th February, pp. 234-261.

Foucault, M. (1991) "Governmentality" in The Foucault Effect: Studies *in Governmentality; With Two Lectures and an Interview with Michel Foucault* Burchell G,Gordon, C and Miller, P (eds.), pp. 87-104, The University of Chicago Press, Chicago.

Frank, A.G. (1978). *Dependent Accumulation and Underdevelopment*, MacMillan Press, London.

Frank, A.G. (1969), *Capitalism and Underdevelopment in Latin America*, Monthly Review Press, New York.

Ghosh, B.N. (1993). "Karl Marx on Development and Underdevelopment", *Indian Economic Journal*, Vol.40, No.4, April-June, pp. 13-23.

Ghosh, B.N. (1997). "Rise, Fall and Resurrection of Political Economy", *Man and Development*, September, pp.36-47.

Giddens, A. (1985). *The Nation State and Violence: A Contemporary Critic of Historical Materialism* Vol. II, Polity Press, Cambridge.

Gohain, H. (1973). "Origin of the Assamese Middle Class", *Social Scientist*, vol.2, no.13, pp.11-26.

Gohain, H. (1980). "Cudgel of Chauvinism", *Economic and Political Weekly*, 23rd February, pp. 419-420.

Gohain, H. (1980). "Fall-Out of Underdevelopment" *Economic and Political Weekly*, 22nd March, pp.589-590.

Gohain, H. (1980). "Tangled Theories", *Economic and Political Weekly*, 19th April, pp.783-785.

Gregory, D. (1994). *Geographical Imaginations*, Blackwell Publication, Cambridge.

Griffin, K (1968). *Underdevelopment In Spanish America*, George Allen and Unwin, London.

Guha, A. (1974). "A Comment on Origins of Assamese Middle Class", *Social Scientist*, vol.2, no. 18-19 (Jan-Feb), pp. 59-66.

Guha, A and Das, A.N. (1977). *Planters- Raj to Swaraj*, ICHR, New Delhi.

Habermas, J. (1977). *On the Logic of Social Sciences*, Polity Press, New York.

Hacking, I. (1991). "How Should We do the History of Statistics?" in Burchell G,Gordon, C and Miller, P (edit) *Governmentality; With Two Lectures and an Interview with Michel Foucaul*,pp.181-196, The University of Chicago Press, Chicago.

Hakli, J. (1994). "Territoriality and the Rise of Modern State", *Fennia*, 172(1), pp.1-82.

Hakli, J. (1994). "Discourse in the Production of Political Space: Decolonizing the Symbolism of Provinces in Finland", *Political Geography*, vol.17, no.3, pp.331-363.

Hall, T.D. (19860). "Incorporation in the World-System: Towards of Critique", *American Sociological Review*, vol.51, pp. 392-402.

Hanna, S.P. (1995). "Finding a Place in the World-Economy: Core-Periphery Relations, the Nation-State and the Underdevelopment of Garret Country, Maryland", *Political Geography*, vol.14, no.5, pp.451-472.

Harley, J.B. (1989). "Deconstructing The Map", *Cartographica*, (26)2, pp.1-20.

Harley, J.B. (1998). "Historical Geography and Cartographical Illusion", *Journal of Historical Geography*, vol.15, pp.80-90.

Harvey, D. (1989). *The Condition of Postmodernity*, Basil Blackwell Publication, Oxford.

Harvey, D. (1993). "From Space to Place and Back Again: Reflections on the Condition of Postmodernity in *Mapping the futures: local cultures, global change*. (Eds: Bird, J., Curtis, B., Putnam, T., Robertson, G., Tickner, L), Routledge, London, pp. 3-29.

Harvey, D. (2000). *The Spaces of Hope*, Edinburgh Press, New York.

Hazarika, N. (1995). "Land Reforms: A Key to Rural Uplift in North-East India, *Yojana,* Annual Number, October, pp.83-86.

Hazarika, S. (2001). "India and its North East: The Challengers of Regionalism and Migration" in Kousar Azam (ed.) *Ethnicity, Identity and State in South Asia*, South Asian Publishers, New Delhi.pp.192-207.

Hussain, M. (1990). "The Nationality Question", *Seminar*, No.366, pp.39-45.

Hussian, M. (1988). *Nagaland: Habitat, Society and Shifting Cultivation*, Rima, New Delhi.

Hussian, M. (2000). "State, Identity Movements and Internal Displacement in the North-East", *Economic and Political Weekly*, 16th December, pp. 4519-4523.

IWGIA. (1998). Year Book, "Nagaland: Ten Months of Peace in 33 Years."

Johnston, R.J. (1991). *A Question of Place: Exploring the Practices of Human Geography*, Basil Blackwell Publications, Oxford.

Karna, M.N. (1990). "The Agrarian Scene", *Seminar*, No.366., pp. 31-37.

Kay, G (1975). *Development and Underdevelopment*, Mac-Millan Press, London.

Khanka, S.S. (1998). "Development of Small Scale Industries in Assam", *Yojana*, September, pp. 41-49.

Knight, D. (1982). "Identity and Territory: Geographical Perspectives on Nationalism and Regionalism", *Annals of Association of American Geographers*, vol.72, Dec, pp. 514-531.

Krishna, S. (2001). "Resources, Communities and Gender Relations: A Study of Arunachal Pradesh", *Indian Journal of Gender Studies*, vol.8.no.2.

Kuri, K.P. (2001). "Usufructuary Mortgage and Land Alienation in Rural Assam", *Man and Development*, Vol.23, No.3, September, pp. 58-63.

Kurian, N.J (2000). "Widening Regional Disparities in India: Some Indicators", *Economic and Political Weekly*, 12 February, pp. 539-550

Latour, B. (1986). "Visualization and Cognition: Thinking With the Eyes and Hands", *Knowledge and Society*, vol. 6.pp.1-40.

Leontyev, L (1960). *Fundamentals of Marxist Political Economy*, Novosti Press Agency Publishing House, Moscow.

Lianzela (1999). "Post Independence Economic Development In Mizoram", *Dialogue*, Vol.1, No.1, July-September.

Madhab, J. (1999). "North-East: Crisis of Identity, Security and Underdevelopment, *Economic and Political Weekly*, 6th February.

Madhab, J. (2000). "Agriculture Key to Development of North-East", *Dialogue*, Vol.2, No.2, Dec.

Manicas, P.T. (1987). *A History and Philosophy of Social Sciences*, Basil Blackwell Publications, Oxford.

Mann, M. (1984). "The Autonomous Power of the State: Its Origin Mechanisms and Results", *Archives euorpennes de socialogie*, xxv,pp. 185-213.

Marx, K. (1938, Third Reprint). *Capital Vol.1*, George Allen and Uniwin, London.

Meher, R. (1999). "Interstate Disparities in Levels of Development and the Implications of Economic Liberalization on Regional Economics of India", *Review of Development and Change*, Vol.4., No.2, July-December, pp. 199-218.

Miri, M. (1996). "Identity, Tribes, Man and Development", in Biaidyanath Sarswati. (ed.), *Interface of Cultural Identity and Development*, IGNCA, New Delhi.

Miri, M. (2003). Identity and the Moral Life, Oxford University Press, New Delhi.

Mishra, D.K. (2001). "The Political Economy of Agrarian Change In Arunachal", *Man and Development*, Vol.23, No.4, September, pp. 40-50.

Mishra, P (2001), *Selective Writing on Society and Polity in NEI*, Communist Party of India, Shillong.

Mishra, S.N.(1983). "Arunachal's Tribal Economic Formations and Their Dissolution", *Economic and Political Weekly*, 22 October, pp. 1837-1845.

Misra, S. (1998 a.). "The Nature of Colonial Intervention in the Naga Hills, 1840-80", *Economic and Political Weekly*, Dec. 19, pp. 3273-3280.

Misra, T. (1980). "Assam: A Colonial Hinterland", *Economic and Political Weekly*, 9th August, pp. 1357-1364.

Misra, U (1980). "Worse than Emergency Days", *Economic and Political Weekly*, 19th April, pp. 731-732.

Misra, U (1988 b.) *North East India: Quest for Identity*, Purbanchal Prakashan, Gauhati.

Misra, U (1998). "Bodo Stir, Complex Issues. Unattainable Demands", *Economic and Political Weekly*, 27.05.98 pp. 1146-1149.

Misra,U.(2000). *The Periphery Strikes Back: Challenges to the Nation-State in Assam and Nagaland*, Indian Institute of Advanced Study, Shimla.

Mitchell, D. (1995). "There is No Such Thing as Culture: Towards a Reconceptualisation of the Idea of Culture", *Transactions of the Institute of British Geographers*, New Series 20,pp.102-116.

Moffat Mills, A.J. (1984). *Report on The Province of Assam*, (first published in 1853), p.246, Guwahati.

Mukhopadhyay, E. (1998). "Arunachal: Illusions of Development", *Man and Development*, December, pp.139-142.

Munshi, S, Guha, A. and Chaube S. (1978). "Regionalisation and Integrated Economic Development In North-East India" in Datta Ray, B. (edit.) *Social and Economic Profile of North-East India*, B.R. Publishing House, New Delhi.

Murphy, A.B. (1991). "Regions As Social Construct: The Gap Between Theory and Practice", *Progress in Human Geography*, vol.15, pp.22-35.

Myrdal, G. (1990), *The Political Element In the Development Of Economic Theory*, Transaction Publishers, New York.

Myrdal, G. (1968). *And Asian Drama: An Inquiry Into the Poverty of Nations, Pantheon, New York.*

Nag, S. (1993). "Multiplications of Nations? Political Economy of Sub-nationalism in India", *Economic and Political Weekly*, 17-24 July.

Narzary, C. (1998). "The Struggle Between Ultras and Moderates", *North East Sun*, Vol.12.No.4.pp.16-18.

Nayar, V.K. (2001), "On the Development Process In the North-East", Dialogue,Vol.3,No.1, July-September,New Delhi.

North Eastern Council. (1995). *Basic Statistics of North East India*, Shillong,

O'Tuathail, G. (1994). "(Dis)placing Geopolitics: Writings on the Maps of Politics", *Environment and Planning D. Society and Space*,vol.12,pp.525-546.

Passi, A (1991). "Deconstructing Regions: Notes on the Scales of Spatial Life", *Environment and Planning A*: 23(2), pp.239.256.

Passi, A. (1986). "The Institutionalization of Regions: A Theoretical Framework for Understanding the Emergence of Regions and Constitutions of Identity", *Fennia*, 164(1), pp. 105-146.

Patel, A.R. (1988), "Developing North-Eastern Region through Banking", *Yojana*, 16-30 November, pp. 19-21.

Patnaik, Prabhat. (1973). "On Political Economy of Underdevelopment", *Economic and Political Weekly*, Annual Number, February, pp. 197-212.

Phukan, U (1983). *Agricultural Development in Assam, 1950-51 to 1984-85,* Mittal Publication, New Delhi.

Phukan, G. (2001) "Ethnic Politics in North- east India: Understanding Elite Conflict and Political Mobilization" in Kousar azam (ed.) *Ethnicity, Identity and State in South Asia*, South Asian Publishers, New Delhi.pp.208-220.

Phukan, G. (2002)(ed.). *Ethnicity and Polity in South Asia*, South Asian Publishers, New Delhi.

Pillai, S.K. (2001). "The Human Factor in the Economy of North-East", *Dialogue*, Vol.3, No.2, October-December.

Planning Commission of India. (2002), *Assam Development Report*, New Delhi.

Porter, T.M. (1986). *The Rise of Statistical Thinking 1820-1900*, Princeton University Press, New Jersey.

Poulantzas, N. (1975). *Class in Contemporary Capitalism*, New Left Press, London.

Prabhakar, M.S. (1973). "The North Eastern Council: Some Political Perspectives", *Economic and Political Weekly*, 6th October, pp. 1823-1826.

Prabhakar, M.S. (1974). "The Politics of a Script: Demand for Acceptance of Roman Script For Bodo Language", *Economic and Political Weekly*, 21st December, pp.2097-2102.

Pred, A. (1984). "Place as Historically Contingent Processes: Strucuration and the Time Geography of Becoming Places", *Annals of the Association of American Geographers*, vol.74, pp.279-297.

Rabinow, P. (1989). *French Modern Norms and Forms of Social Environment*, MIT Press, Cambridge.

Rana, P.B and Mohapatra, P.P.(1992). "Tea and Money versus the Human Life: The Rise and Fall of the Indenture System in the Assam Tea Plantation 1840-1908", Jouranl of Peasant Studies, vol.19, no. ¾ (April/July), pp.142-172.

Rao, M.G., Shah, R.T. and, K.P. Kalirajan. (1999). "Convergence Incomes Across Indian States", *Economic and Political Weekly*, 27 March, pp. 769-778.

Revel, J (1991). "Knowledge of the Territory", *Science in Context*, 4(1), 133-161.

Rostow, W.W. (1971,2nd edition). *Stages of Economic Growth*, Cambridge University Press, Cambridge.

Routledge, P. (1992). "Putting Politics in its Place: Balipal, India, as a Terrain of Resistance", *Political Geography*, vol.11, no.6, pp.588-611.

RoyBurman, B.K. (1989). "Problems and Prospects of Tribal Development", *Economic and Political Weekly*, 1 April, pp 693-697.

RoyBurman, B.K. (1990). "Land and Forest Rights", *Seminar*, No.366, pp.25-29.

RoyBurman, B.K (1999). "Federalism, Globalism and Pattern of Sharing Rights and Responsibilities with Particular Reference to Assam and the Federal Polity of India, *Dialogue*, Vol.1, No.1.

Ruccio, F.D. and Simon, H.L. (1986). "Methodological Aspects of a Marxian Approach to Development: An Analysis of the Modes of Production", *World Development*, vol.14, no.2, pp.211-222.

Ruggie, J. G. (1993)."Territoriality and Beyond Problematizing Modernity In International Relations", *International Organization*, 47(1), 139-174.

Sachdeva, G. (2000). *Economy of the North East: Policy, Present Conditions and Future Possibilities*, Konark Publications Limited, New Delhi.

Sack, R.D. (1986). *Human Territoriality: Its Theory and History*, Cambridge University Press, Cambridge.

Sahni, A. (2000). "The Terrorist Economy in India's Northeast: Preliminary Exploration" paper presented at the Indian Council for Social Science Research (March 2-3), India International Center, New Delhi.

Saikia, P.D. & D. Borah. (1992). *Constraints of Economic Development of North- East India*, Omsons Publication, New Delhi.

Sarkar, A.N. (1993). "Planning Integrated Development of the North-East", *Yojana*,15 December, pp. 26-28.

Sarkar, P.C. (1994). "Regional Imbalances in Indian Economy over Plan Periods", *Economic and Political Weekly*, 12 March, pp. 621-633.

Sau, R. (1975). "Capitalism, Imperialism and Underdevelopment", *Economic and Political Weekly*, Special Number, August, pp. 1267-1275.

Sau, R. (1975). "The Dialectics of Underdevelopment", *Economic and Political Weekly*, 5 July, pp. 999-1004.

Scott, J. (1999). *The Cultural Economy of the Cities*, University of California Press, Los Angeles.

Scott, J. (2000) "Hill and Valley in South-east Asia ....Why the State is the Enemy of the People Who Move Around...or..Why Civilisation Don't Climb Hills", paper presented at symposium on Development and the Nation-State, Washington University, St.Luis.http///www.artsci.wsutl.edu/~symp2000/scott.PDF

Sen, S. (1986). *Arunachal Pradesh and the Tribes: A Selected Bibliography*, Gyan Publishing House, New Delhi.

Sharma J, N. (1966). "Problems of economic Development in Assam" in *Economic and Political Weekly, vol.* No.1. Issue No.7.

Sharma, M. (1990). *Social and Economic Change in Assam: Middle Class Hegemony*, Ajanta Publications, Delhi.

Shields, R. (1999). *Lefebvre Love and Struggle: Spatial Dialectics*, pp.141-189, Routledge, New York.

Shukla, G.P. and Haridasan, K(1996). "Ethnoforestry", *Arunachal Pradesh Forest News*, vol.141, pp.20-24.

Sikdar, S. (1982). "Tribalism Vs. Colonialism British Capitalistic Intervention and Transformation of Primitive Economy of Arunachal

Pradesh in Nineteenth Century", *Social Scientist*, v.10, no.115 Dec.pp.15-31.

Singh, B.P. (2001). "The Eastern Himalaya: Wetlands, Forests and Beliefs", *Man and Development*, Vol.23, No.4, December,pp. 76-92.

Singh, B.P. (1996), *Problems of Change*, New Delhi, Oxford University Press.

Singh, L.P. (1990). "Problem the North-East: A Symposium On the Problems of a Neglected People and Region", *Seminar*, No.366, February, pp. 12-18.

Sinha, A.C. (1998). "Agenda For Co-Operation Between India's North-East and Its Neighbouring Countries", *Man and Development*, December, pp. 143-156.

Sircar, K.K. (1986). "A Tale of Two Boards: Some Early Management Problems of Assam Limited, 1839-1864", *Economic and Political Weekly*, 8-15 March, pp. 453-459.

Smith, N. (1990). *Uneven Development: Nature, Capital and the Reproduction of Space*, Blackwell Publications, and Oxford.

Soja, E. (1971). "The Political Organization of Space", *Washington Association of American Geographers*, Resource Paper No. 8.

Sweezy, P. and Magdoff, H. (1989). *Irreversible Crisis*, Monthly Review Press, New York.

Taylor, P.J. (1991). "A Theory and Practice of Regions: The Case of Europe", *Environment and Planning D: Society and Space*, vol.9, pp.183-195.

Thomas, C. (1976). *Dependence and Transformation*, Monthly Review Press, NewYork.

Thrift, N. (1983). "On the Determination of Social Action in Space and Time", *Environment and Planning D: Society and Space*, vol. 1, 23-57.

Thrift, N. (1994). "Taking Aim at the Heart of Region" in Gregory, D., Martin, R., and Smith, G (edit.) *Human Geography: Soceity, Space and Social Science*, pp.200-221, University of Minnesota Press, Minneapolis.

Urry, J. (1987). "Society, Space and Locality", *Environment and Planning D: Society and Space*, vol.5, pp.435-444.

Verghese,B.G.(1995). *The Resurgent North East India*, Konark Publishers, New Delhi.

Wagner, P. (1989). "Social Science and the State in Continental Western Europe: The Political Structuration of Disciplinary Discourse", *International Social Science Journal*, no.22, and pp.509-528.

Wallerstein, I. and Martin, W. (1979). Peripheralization of Southern Africa, II, Changes in Household Strucure and Labour-force Formation, *Review*: 3, pp. 193-207.

Weiner, M. (1993). "Political Demography of Assam's Anti Immigrant Movement", *Population and Development Review*, Vol.9, No.2, June, pp. 279-292.

Weaver, J and Berger, M. (1984). "The Marxist Critique of Dependency Theory: An Introduction" in Wilber, C.K. (edit.) *The Political Economy of Development and Underdevelopment*, pp. 45-64, Random House Inc, New York.

William, C and Smith A.D. (1983). "The National Construction of Social Space", *Progress In Human Geography*, vol.7, pp. 502-518.

Wittrock, B. (1989). "Social Science and the State of Development of Transformations of Discourse of Modernity", *International Social Science Journal*, no.22, pp. 497-508.

Index